SO THIS IS FAITH

BECOMING AN AUTHENTIC DISCIPLE OF CHRIST

KEVIN STIRRATT

BEACON HILL PRESS
OF KANSAS CITY

Copyright 2007
By Kevin Stirratt and Beacon Hill Press of Kansas City

ISBN-13: 978-0-8341-2303-8
ISBN-10: 0-8341-2303-7

Cover Design: Brandon R. Hill
Interior Design: Sharon Page

Library of Congress Cataloging-in-Publication Data

Stirratt, Kevin, 1967-
  So this is faith : becoming an authentic disciple of Christ / Kevin Stirratt.
    p. cm.
  Includes bibliographical references.
  ISBN-13: 978-0-8341-2303-8 (pbk.)
  ISBN-10: 0-8341-2303-7 (pbk.)
  1. Spiritual formation. 2. Spirituality. 3. Spiritual life—Christianity. 4. Christian life. I. Title.

  BV4511.S75 2007
  248.4—dc22

2007007983

10 9 8 7 6 5 4 3 2 1

CONTENTS

ACKNOWLEDGMENTS

I want to express special thanks to Nancy Kupfersmith, who painstakingly edited both the student and leader's guides. Her work was selfless and relentless. I also want to express gratitude to the many groups who served as guinea pigs over the last several years as this material has been developed and refined.

HOW TO USE THIS STUDY

This study will guide you as you grow in your relationship with God. It begins by reviewing several key things Christians believe about God and our relationship with Him through His Son, Jesus. With that foundation, the study then turns to helping you make weekly progress toward getting to know God better and strengthening your friendship with Him.

STUDY LAYOUT

The first section is called Revisiting the Foundations (chapters 1 to 2). Chapter 1 will recall what the Bible teaches about God, humanity, and the relationships God intended for us to have with Him and each other. It will then review the effect of natural selfishness, or sin, on our relationships with God and others. Chapter 2 highlights what the Bible teaches about God's solution to the most basic human problems. It reminds us how Jesus restored life to our broken and dying relationships with God and each other.

The second section, Rebuilding a Friendship with God (chapters 3 to 7), explores some of the ways we move beyond knowing *about* God to truly *knowing* God. While section one discusses what God did to restore our relationship with Him, section two outlines some of the ways we build that relationship. Prayer, Bible study, personal worship, and spiritual sensitivity are at the heart of this section.

The third and fourth sections, Restoring His Image, Parts I and II (chapters 8 to 15), cover the final part of the study. They discuss the ways God restores His image in us. In these two sections you will discover God's real purpose in sending Jesus to us. God wants our character restored to be like His. These sections focus on the introduction to one of Jesus' most famous sermons, in which He lays out what a truly blessed life looks like (Matthew 5, the Beatitudes). Each blessing says something about the restoration of God's character in us.

We were created to look like God in our character. But selfishness and poor choices damaged His image in us—breaking our relationships with God and others. For 2,000 years Jesus has fixed these problems and restored millions to the vital, healthy relationships they were meant to enjoy.

CHAPTER LAYOUT

Jesus taught us that God the Father seeks worshipers who worship Him in spirit and truth (John 4:24). While some studies tend to look at only the truths of Scripture, our purpose is to help you get to know God better and find new and deeper ways to worship Him. To do this, each chapter contains four sections: *Truth, Questions to Consider, Spirit,* and *Spiritual Journey Journal.*

TRUTH

Each chapter begins by outlining truths in Scripture and related research through a series of stories and Bible study.

QUESTIONS TO CONSIDER

This section contains thought-provoking questions to help you evaluate the ideas in the Truth section and apply them to you and your relationship with God.

SPIRIT

The Spirit section will help you become more sensitive to God and His leading. The Bible teaches us that if we draw near to God, He will draw near to us (James 4:8). The Spirit section will guide you through talking with God, reading the Bible, serving others, worshiping, and evaluating your spiritual journey.

SPIRITUAL JOURNEY JOURNAL

The Spiritual Journey Journal will follow the Spirit section. Many people find it helpful to record their thoughts and ideas. The Journal section will help you track your progress along the way. It will guide you as you create a record of your journey and your discoveries. Journaling is a way for you to record thoughts, refine questions, and capture insights. As you read the chapters, explore the Scripture, and open yourself to God's leading, the journal is a place to reflect on what is happening in your spiritual journey.

As the weeks progress, the Spirit section and the Spiritual Journey Journal will help you make the most of your spiritual journey.

As you progress, you will have opportunities to take some exciting risks by following where you sense God is leading you. As you do this, you may want to share your journey with other seekers as part of the community known as the church.

Your Spiritual Journey Journal is private. If you are using this material in a class or small-group setting, you need only share insights from your journal that you choose to share. You will *never* be asked to share your spiritual journal if you don't want to, so feel free to be honest and real with yourself and God.

HOW TO FIND MATERIAL IN THE BIBLE

If you are new to Bible study, keep in mind that the Bible is a collection of 66 books, a miniature library. It could be difficult and confusing to find anything in it if it did not have an easy-to-use indexing system. Years ago, people on spiritual journeys like yours decided they needed a way to find ideas and sections quickly. The 66 books of the Bible were numbered to make it easy for people to find their way around. This is called a Bible reference.

A Bible reference may look confusing at first. Each reference has different parts. Here's an example of a Bible reference:

John 3:16

This reference points to one sentence in the Bible in the book called the Gospel of John. The first part of the reference always tells the book in the Bible. In this case it is John. If you aren't sure where to find a book, simply open your Bible to the table of contents. You will find all the books listed in two sections: the Old Testament and the New Testament. Each Testament has several books in it. The Old Testament has books written before Jesus. The New Testament has books written after Jesus died. It covers Jesus' life and the early years of the Church.

The table of contents lists the books in each Testament in the order they appear in the Bible. The page number tells where that book begins in your Bible.

In a Bible reference, a number usually follows the book name. That number refers to the chapter in the book. In this example, the chapter is 3. When a colon follows the chapter, the number or numbers that follow identify a verse or verses within the chapter. In the example, the verse is 16.

John 3:16 means the Book of John, chapter 3, and the 16th verse.

Here's another example:

John 3:16-17

This is similar to our first example, but it includes more verses. It means the Book of John, chapter 3, verses 16 through 17. This is helpful when you want to find or keep track of several verses. A hyphen means *through*. A comma between verses means *and*.

CLASS/SMALL-GROUP MEETINGS

If you are using this material in a class, discipleship course, or small-group setting, you can expect an open atmosphere.* The leader will respect you and your questions and honor your current place in your spiritual journey. You

---

*A leader's guide for this study can be found online at <www.beaconhill books.com>.

may be encouraged to participate in the community of the church. Don't feel any pressure to share anything you don't want to. However, the more open you allow yourself to become, the more you will get out of your spiritual journey.

Each group time will begin with some type of ice-breaker. These are fun and thought-provoking exercises designed to get you thinking about the various issues the chapter addresses. Each week the class facilitator will ask the group for prayer requests. This is a time for you to begin enjoying the prayer support of others who are also traveling on their spiritual journeys. You may find it uncomfortable to share personal prayer requests at first. Don't worry. You will never be forced into anything. However, the more you are willing to risk this small act of vulnerability, the more you will be opening yourself to God's presence. As you are comfortable doing so, ask those in your group to pray for you, your family, and your spiritual journey.

To help everyone feel comfortable and know what to expect, the group times will follow these ground rules.

1. All questions are welcome and will not be shot down by the facilitator or other class members. We must all agree that no matter how uncomfortable a question might make us feel, or how much we might disagree with the premise behind a question, we will respect the rights of the people in this class to ask whatever they wish to ask without fear of rejection.

2. You do not have to speak or share if you do not want to, even though we encourage all to speak up with insights or questions. We gain more by active participation.

3. The purpose for this class is to help you grow in your relationship with God. His Spirit will be with you, guiding you in your reading, study, and group discussion. It is important to be alert to what His Spirit is saying.

4. The course is Wesleyan in its theological heritage. Basically, that means the course assumes people are created in God's image. However, that likeness has been seriously damaged and distorted. We are born selfish. We are made righteous in Christ. We are born loving ourselves. The Holy Spirit enables us to love God and others. This transformation is possible because Jesus came to restore the divine image. God is ready to forgive the wrong things people do and to restore His creation through Christ's forgiveness and the Holy Spirit's power.

RECOMMENDATIONS FOR FURTHER STUDY

The spiritual disciplines taught throughout the various chapters are widely used disciplines discussed by many authors on the subject of spiritual formation. There are many volumes of material available to those who would seek to develop this part of their spiritual journey more fully.

It is my prayer that as you invest yourself in the weeks to come, you will draw close to God and find the relationship with Him that will satisfy the very core of your being.

REVISITING THE FOUNDATIONS

ONE

OUR RELATIONSHIP WITH GOD AND EACH OTHER

TRUTH

Before we find out how to develop our friendship with God, we need to recall a few things about Him, ourselves, and His Son, Jesus. That's what this chapter and the next are going to do, bring some key things to mind that we may know but could use a quick refreshing in. So to start off, let's take a look at God and some important things we need to remember about Him.

We know God is the Creator of the universe and all that's in it. That's what Genesis, the first book of the Bible, says. But God is also holy; that means He is separate from His creation and special in His character. God relates to us according to His special character. Yet sometimes we only see part of His holiness and miss the rest.

My six-year-old looked at me one time after I intervened in his life and said, "Dad, you're mean." In his mind my disciplining to redirect his behavior displaced my love for him. He didn't see that I disciplined him because I loved him and wanted him to live a good life. He was doing what we often do with God, seeing the discipline minus His love—a key part of God's holy character.

God disciplines us because He loves us and wants us to grow up to be as He is. He tells us in chapter 19 of Leviticus that He is holy and that we are to reflect this in our own lives. In verse 18 He describes what that looks like—"love your neighbor as yourself." He wants us to be holy as He is by loving as He loves.

First John 1:9 then says, "If we confess our sins, he is faithful and just and will forgive us our sins and purify us from all unrighteousness." The root word for *righteousness* can also be translated *justice*. God seeks to restore our ability not only to love but also to embrace godly justice.

So in these verses, God shows us that His holy character is a balance of love and justice. He wants our lives to reflect that balance of love and justice. Some people only see God as just and emphasize the rules. Others lose sight of the justice and see God as a heavenly pushover, to whom almost anything is acceptable. But God's discipline and love work hand-in-hand. He expresses His love to us through His discipline, hoping to renew His character in us.

When we look at the first three chapters of Genesis, we find that God originally wanted us to be like Him. Genesis 1:26 says, "Let us make man in our image." Yet somehow things didn't work out the way He intended. We all have an idea about what happened, but let's review it so we can get a look at the complete picture.

God created humankind to be a balance of love and justice, just as He is, but He also gave humans the freedom to choose how they wanted to live. They could choose to love and obey God or do otherwise. All that was needed was one simple command to obey for this freedom to be used. So God told the first humans, Adam and Eve, that they could eat any fruit except the fruit of one tree.

Adam and Eve chose to disobey God, and this changed everything. The intimate friendship with God we were created to enjoy was changed to fear, shame, and distrust. Human relationships were seriously damaged. Adam and Eve shifted from love and partnership to blame and shame. Humanity, no longer reflecting the image of God, was now marred with selfishness and all the destructiveness that goes with it.

Scripture teaches us that we are all affected by Adam and Eve's sin. As Romans 5 makes clear, Adam is our ancestor, and through him sin entered the world. We are born looking like our fathers and their fathers and their fathers all the way back to Adam. Because of this, we enter the world unable to fully love God, as Romans 6—8 explains. We want what we want, and we easily fall into acts of rebellion, or sin. We know what is right but don't do it. We know what is wrong and leap at the chance.

Genesis 6:5 is shockingly honest about our absolute selfishness. "The LORD saw how great man's wickedness on the earth had become, and that every inclination of the thoughts of his heart was only evil all the time." It is no wonder that the Bible talks about our need to be reborn. We are born in such rebellion to God that something radical needs to happen if we are to ever have a relationship with God where we again are "in his image."

Now we know God did something very special through His Son, Jesus, that took care of this mess humankind found itself in. We'll look again in more detail at what Jesus did in the next chapter. In the meantime, we can see in our own lives the result of what God did through Jesus. He reclaimed us through His Son—we've been reborn. We may still struggle with temptations, and our selfishness may surface now and then, but we can confess our sins just as 1 John 1:9 says, and God will forgive us. In many ways God is restoring us to the image of holiness—the balance of love and justice—that He intended at the beginning.

Our problem once we know God through Jesus is that we do not always go to God and admit we are tempted and confess when we sin. Sometimes we blame people or things for our failings. We mess up and yell, "He did it!" We refuse to admit that the problem with sin lies with us. Yet this is exactly what James 1:13-15 teaches:

> When tempted, no one should say, "God is tempting me." For God cannot be tempted by evil, nor does he tempt anyone; but each one is tempted when, by his own evil desire, he is dragged away and enticed. Then, after desire has conceived, it gives birth to sin; and sin, when it is full-grown, gives birth to death.

There is no doubt that temptation is an inside job. This is the effect of Adam's sin in us. We hide from God when we should run to Him in honest confession about what is happening. Although it's not a sin to be tempted, if we don't go to God for help right away, sin is just what we may end up committing. Openness with God is so very important. We need His Holy Spirit to step in and strengthen us when we're tempted. And if we do sin, we certainly need to confess this to God so He can forgive us and restore our relationship with Him.

At the heart of God's plan for us is freedom from being controlled by our own self-centered nature. When we give in to temptation and commit sin, we need to return to the One who loves us so we can again have this freedom.

All this may seem very simple, but it's not. God provided this wonderful plan at a great cost. John 3:16 sums up how far God's love was willing to go to bring us back into an intimate relationship with Him: "For God so loved the world that he gave his one and only Son, that whoever believes in him shall not perish but have eternal life."

God opened the way for us to be friends with Him again. And He did this at the cost of His Son. Jesus was the priceless bridge God provided back to himself. That's what we will refresh our minds about next. We will look at who Jesus is and review what He did to restore our friendship with God and each other and set us on the path of renewing God's image in us.

QUESTIONS TO CONSIDER

1. Most people tend to emphasize either God's love or His justice. Which do you tend to emphasize? How does this impact the way you re-

late to God? In what ways do you need to balance your understanding of God's holiness?

2. How did Adam's relationship with God change after Adam sinned? Do you see any of these traits in your own relationship with God?

3. How did Adam and Eve's relationship change after they sinned? Do you see any similarities with the problems men and women face today in their relationships?

4. How does it make you feel to understand that you aren't able to overcome your own selfishness on a consistent basis? What do you think this means for you and your spiritual journey? Where do you need God to help you the most to avoid demanding your own way?

5. God is willing to forgive. Can you think of areas in your life that you have not confessed? Since God is willing to forgive, why do you think peo-

ple try to hide their sin? What might be a better way of dealing with sin?

SPIRIT

Breath Prayers

Jesus taught us that God seeks people who worship Him in spirit and truth. Each chapter will include the previous section for sorting through the truths being explored. However, getting to know God better includes not only the mind but also the spirit. So each chapter will also include some helps to increase your openness to God's presence.

One way we can begin to be sensitive to God's leading is through the use of *breath prayers*. A breath prayer is a word or phrase that we repeat to keep ourselves focused on God and sensitive to His presence. A breath prayer can summarize or apply a biblical truth. This week use Jeremiah 29:11 as the inspiration for the following breath prayer:

> "For I know the plans I have for you," declares the LORD, "plans to prosper you and not to harm you, plans to give you hope and a future."

Sample Breath Prayer: "I am laying my hope and future on You, God."

Whenever your mind turns to God and you search for Him, say this simple breath prayer. You may be surprised how encouraging this prayer can be.

SPIRITUAL JOURNEY JOURNAL

WEEK 1

Take some time daily to record any thoughts or spiritual insights you have about God. Begin each day by reading the scripture passage listed. Try to write a short breath prayer from the passage to use throughout the day. In the evening, record your thoughts, insights, and any ways you found God calling you to transformation during the day. Whether you discover an attitude that needs changing or something deeply spiritual that must be addressed, embrace it and praise God for showing it to you. God trusts you to obey Him in this area.

Monday

Scripture: Genesis 1:26-29
Breath Prayer:

Self-Evaluation—God's call to transformation:

Tuesday

Scripture: Genesis 3:1-10
Breath Prayer:

Self-Evaluation—God's call to transformation:

Wednesday

Scripture: Romans 5:12
Breath Prayer:

Self-Evaluation—God's call to transformation:

Thursday

    Scripture: Romans 8:6-9

    Breath Prayer:

Self-Evaluation—God's call to transformation:

Friday

    Scripture: Genesis 6:5-6

    Breath Prayer:

Self-Evaluation—God's call to transformation:

Saturday

    Scripture: Galatians 5:16-17

    Breath Prayer:

Self-Evaluation—God's call to transformation:

Sunday

    Before leaving for church, read today's scripture passage, write out and pray your breath prayer, and ask God to draw near to you. Use the sections below to guide you on this Sabbath Day as you worship and spend time with God.

    Scripture: 2 Corinthians 3:12-18

    Breath Prayer:

Insights from Sunday School/Bible Study/Small-Group Time:

Preparing for Worship:

    During worship, I need You to do this in my heart . . .

As I come to worship, I need You to know . . .

Insights from Worship:

Reflecting on this Sabbath . . .

Today, God, You showed me . . .

This week I want You to do this in my heart . . .

Self-Evaluation—God's call to transformation:

REBUILDING A BRIDGE TO GOD

TRUTH

Children have a way of asking questions that seem simple. Yet, when we try to answer the question, we realize it isn't as simple as it seems. I think the simplest and most complex question a child has ever asked me is, "Who is Jesus?" Try explaining that one in two sentences or less! The answer to the question is at the heart of rebuilding a relational bridge to God. Some of humankind's most profound questions are answered by the response to that child's question.

Much of what we know about Jesus comes from the writings of those who walked and talked with Him. We can revisit what they wrote about Him in the New Testament. John 1:1-4 even says something about Jesus' beginnings before His birth:

> In the beginning was the Word, and the Word was with God, and the Word was God. He was with God in the beginning. Through him all things were made; without him nothing was made that has been made. In him was life, and that life was the light of men.

The first statement by John echoes Genesis 1:1, "In the beginning was God." John is intentionally reflecting the creation account here. This isn't about the beginning of Jesus' life on earth but about the beginning of all things. This begins with God—the Word. John uses Genesis 1:1 to clarify the identity of the God who created all things. He is the Logos.

Logos is a word that was used in John's day to explain the apparent order in the universe. *Logos* is often translated "Word," as in John 1:1. It is closely related to the words *reason* and *order*. John is saying to his audience, "You know this order you see and call 'Logos'? I know Him. I have walked with Him. I know His name!"

I tried to explain this to my six-year-old son, who needed to be reassured that Jesus would be present with him while he slept alone in his room at night. I told him to look at his hand and to take a deep breath. I then said, "The Bible says that it is Jesus who keeps you breathing and lets your body work. In fact, He is the reason your whole body stays together. If He wasn't there, you would just fall into a million billion pieces. So, if you wake up and feel frightened, take a breath and look at your hand. If you are still breathing and your body is still together, you know that Jesus is still there. There's no reason to be afraid."

The success of this little talk was confirmed several months later when my son declared one morning, "Dad! I woke up this morning and I was still here! And I said to myself, 'Jesus is still here!'" He had learned the very important lesson that Jesus, as the Logos, is the force that holds all life together.

Everything that has been made has been made through Jesus—the Word, the Logos. Genesis 1 hints at this idea. Every time God creates, He does so through the spoken word. It is His design, His order, that brings things into existence. It is like the sign on a church I once read: "We believe in the Big Bang theory. God spoke . . . BANG!" Regardless of how you explain the universe, it all begins with Jesus.

The apostle John caps this revelation about the true identity of Jesus with a very interesting statement, "In him was life" (John 1:4). At the heart of Jesus' identity as the Logos, Creator and Sustainer of the universe, is His ability to bring life out of nothing. This reality is the light, the hope, of all men. He is the One who is the Author of life.

Considering the eternal implications of our sinfulness—death and separation from God, Jesus' ability to bring life is our true hope. At the heart of His character is this ability to restore us from the effect of sin, to bring life where there was death. His life, death, and resurrection all serve as avenues Jesus uses to bring about this rebirth.

Now that we've looked at Jesus' prebirth identity, let's recall some of what we know about His earthly life. We know from the Gospels that His mother was Mary and that an angel had appeared to her and announced His birth (see Luke 1). What is most astounding is that Mary was a virgin and that the angel said, "The Holy Spirit will come upon you, and the power of the Most High will overshadow you. So the holy one to be born will be called the Son of God" (v. 35). Jesus would not have a human father!

Why would God send a child born of a virgin? Remember how Adam's sin affected all those born after him?

Everyone has a tendency to rebel, to act on an inner self-centeredness. Changing this situation would require someone without this self-centered tendency—someone blameless who could be the sacrifice for the sins of the whole earth. Being conceived by the Holy Spirit and born of a virgin, Jesus was free from the selfish taint arising from Adam's original disobedience.

Philippians 2 tell us more. From the beginning, as John 1 implies in the discussion about the Logos, Jesus was God. But He didn't consider His equality with God—His Godly glory—a thing to be grasped (the word means "clung to," like a mother clinging to a child in a storm). In God's plan to provide for our forgiveness and cleansing, Jesus emptied himself of His glory; He became human but did not stop being God.

Understanding what the Scripture means when it says Jesus emptied himself (v. 8) has resulted in much discussion through the centuries. Jesus helped clarify this by continually maintaining His identity as God. He said, "Anyone who has seen me has seen the Father" (John 14:9). Yet Jesus emptied himself of His power, becoming dependent on the Father for all He did (see Luke 10:20). That's why Jesus' miracles didn't begin until John baptized Him and a voice from heaven declared, "This is my Son, whom I love; with him I am well pleased" (Matthew 3:17). Jesus needed rest and spiritual feeding. He went into the wilderness to be alone and pray. When Philippians 2:7 says, "being made in human likeness," it means Jesus became a man, not that He became *like* a man.

So Jesus is fully God and fully man. He is the God-man. John 1:14 sums this up: "The Word became flesh and made his dwelling among us. We have seen his glory, the glory of the One and Only, who came from the Father, full of grace and truth."

As the God-man, Jesus is the bridge that spans the gulf between God and us. He was free from the effect of Adam's sin. He lived life as we do and could still be tempted, but He chose to obey the Father in every way, even to His death. God planned things this way. God, in the person of His Son, loved us enough to be the One to provide the sacrifice for our sins. Jesus' life, death, and resurrection show God's holiness. Love sent Jesus as a baby. Justice was satisfied by His sacrificial death. Because Jesus fulfilled the plan, the Father raised Him from the dead and restored Him to His full glory so we could believe and enjoy the relationship God created us to have. This is the Good News, the plan of salvation.

Remember how sin created a divorce in our relationship with God? Hiding and fear replaced closeness and intimacy when Adam and Eve sinned. Our human relationships were also disrupted. Shame and blame poisoned our relationships with each other. But now Jesus has given us an "abundant" life (John 10:10) and things have changed. Through Him we have a way to repair our relationship with God and transform our relationships with others from selfishness to serving.

By lovingly and obediently living a sinless life and dying on the Cross, Jesus released us from the punishment we deserve for our sins. Romans 6:23 says the wages we earn when we sin is death. Because Adam sinned and we each selfishly choose to sin, we earn the ultimate death penalty. But now Jesus has suffered for us and made forgiveness from God possible. We now have the promise of resurrection and eternal life. When we confess our sins to God and ask Him to forgive us and lead us, God applies Jesus' sacrifice to us. Our sin is forgiven, and forgiveness clears the way for us to have a relationship with God both now and for eternity. As the apostle Paul says, "God was reconciling the world to himself in Christ, not counting men's sins against them" (2 Corinthians 5:19).

Jesus not only made friendship with God possible but also opened the way to repairing our ruined relationships with other people. He sent the Holy Spirit to overcome the selfishness that keeps us focused on ourselves and prevents us from fully loving God. But the by-product of a full love for God is the ability to fully love others. So when the Spirit controls the way we think and act, He transforms our behavior and relationships. The Holy Spirit enables us to fulfill Jesus' command to "love your neighbor as yourself" (Matthew 22:39).

When we look at the complete picture, we find that what Jesus has done for us is priceless. He died for our sins and paid the cost for our rebellion. He gave us a way to know God as a friend. He put His Spirit in us so that what comes out of us would be loving instead of self-centered. He made it possible for us to have a whole new set of loving relationships with God and other people.

We should now have fresh in our minds s
things about God, His Son, and ourselves. Wh
reviewed in this chapter and the one before it are .
foundations upon which a friendship with God is built.
The next few chapters are about building that friendship
and exploring what it's like. They will not explain everything about knowing God; that would be a project with no
end. But they will discuss some helpful ways to enrich and
deepen our relationship with Him.

QUESTIONS TO CONSIDER

1. What kinds of order do you see in the world around you? How does it make you feel to know Jesus himself keeps all things running smoothly?

2. How would you have felt if you had been able to walk and talk with Jesus knowing that He is the Creator of the universe? When we ask Christ to come into our lives, forgive our sins, and lead us, He comes into us through the Holy Spirit. How does it make you feel to know you *do* walk with Jesus, the God-man?

3. How do you think Jesus dealt with temptations differently because He didn't have Adam's selfishness? What evidence do you see in Scripture that Jesus' temptations were real and genuinely tempting to Him?

4. If you were Jesus, how would you respond to someone who said, "You don't understand me"?

5. If you could develop a friendship with God, what would you want it to be like? What do you think God wants from a friendship with you? What steps can you take to begin building your friendship with God?

6. Write a prayer to tell God how you feel about what Jesus did for you. What do you think you need to do to draw closer to Him? What do you want God to do through you? Where do you need God's help?

SPIRIT

Praying the Scripture

One of the most powerful spiritual disciplines is praying the Scriptures. You have already started this through the breath prayers you prayed last week. This week we will learn how to use Scripture as the basis for a longer prayer. You will use your Bible as the source of your prayer during your personal worship time. Using Scripture as your source of prayer incorporates the power of God's Word into your prayers.

This technique for praying is simple and yet wonderful. Follow this pattern. Once you are comfortable with it, feel free to adjust it to find the way that works best for you.

1. Begin by taking time to focus your thoughts and feelings on God. You may try prayer, music, or silence.

2. Start reading the Bible passage you've chosen.

3. When something seems important and stands out to you, such as a lesson, insight, or impression from the Holy Spirit, stop and pray about it. Ask God to help you put whatever you have learned into practice. This may mean that you need to change whatever behavior you recognize is outside of God's ways. Thank God that He is going to help you. If the insight was something about God's person or character, stop and praise Him for His greatness. Jesus taught His disciples to begin prayers this way, "Our Father in heaven, hallowed [holy or reverenced] be your name."

4. Take a minute to be silent. Listen for God's voice. Is He giving you instruction, affirmation, or further insight? Continue this dialogue until you feel satisfied that you have experienced God and met with Him. Then move back into the Scripture.

5. Continue this process of reading and praying until you reach the end of the section you've set aside to read today or reached the end of your allotted time. You may find that you may move a little more slowly as you allow God to teach you as you read and pray. That's OK. The goal is to draw closer to God, not to finish a passage. Take your time. Enjoy this intimate time of fellowship with God.

There is something powerful about inviting God to show himself through His Word and then taking the time to allow Him to do that. Follow these times with prayer, asking God to help you with what He has shown you. Once you begin these close dialogues with God and sense His presence and leading, it will be hard to imagine there was a time when you wondered if He was really there. You will discover that God is not just some force out there. He is right here with us.

SPIRITUAL JOURNEY JOURNAL

WEEK 2

Before you dive into your Spiritual Journey Journal this week, establish a place and a time for personal worship. Once you've decided where, when, and how often, make sure you write this into your calendar. Protect your time with God as you would any other scheduled meeting.

Begin each day this week by reading the scripture passage listed. Try to write a short breath prayer from the passage to use throughout the day. In the evening record your thoughts, insights, and any ways you found God calling you to transformation during the day. Whatever the needed transformation is, embrace it and praise God for showing it to you.

Be sure to try out the different spiritual disciplines introduced each week in the Spirit section. You may find the praying the Scriptures option taught today to be a very intimate and special way to spend time with God. Before long you will develop a personal approach to connecting with God that incorporates those practices that work best for you.

My Place for Personal Worship Is . . .

My Time(s) for Personal Worship Is (Are) . . .

Monday

　　Scripture: John 1:1-4
　　Breath Prayer:

Self-Evaluation—God's call to transformation:

Tuesday

　　Scripture: Luke 1:30-35
　　Breath Prayer:

Self-Evaluation—God's call to transformation:

Wednesday

> Scripture: Philippians 2:5-11
> Breath Prayer:

Self-Evaluation—God's call to transformation:

Thursday

> Scripture: John 10:10 and Romans 6:23
> Breath Prayer:

Self-Evaluation—God's call to transformation:

Friday

> Scripture: Hebrews 2:14-18; 4:15; 5:7-10; and
> 1 John 1:9
> Breath Prayer:

Self-Evaluation—God's call to transformation:

Saturday

> Scripture: Matthew 5:17 and 22:34-40
> Breath Prayer:

Self-Evaluation—God's call to transformation:

Sunday

> Before leaving for church, read today's scripture passage, write out and pray your breath prayer, and ask God to draw near to you. Use the sections below to guide you on this Sabbath Day as you worship and spend time with God.

Scripture: John 16:7-15; Romans 8:5; and Galatians 5:13-26

Breath Prayer:

Insights from Sunday School/Bible Study/Small-Group Time:

Preparing for Worship:

During worship, I need You to do this in my heart . . .

As I come to worship, I need You to know . . .

Insights from Worship:

Reflecting on this Sabbath . . .

Today, God, You showed me . . .

This week I want You to do this in my heart . . .

Self-Evaluation—God's call to transformation:

BUILDING A FRIENDSHIP WITH GOD

THREE

FEAR OR LOVE?
HOW WILL WE RELATE?

TRUTH

One of the greatest gifts God gives is friendship with our parents. As children, we go through several phases in our relationships with our parents. Each stage convinces parents and children alike they will never survive. The challenges of growing a relationship are enormous.

We begin our journey completely unaware of the power that is hidden within the mommy. However, it doesn't take long before our self-centered understanding of this world collides with the reality that mom and dad are bigger and wield the power.

My earliest memories of discipline are full of the sense of injury. One day my brother and I sneaked the Apple Jacks breakfast cereal to the top of the stairs that led to our bedroom. In our covert operation, we had found victory over the inspecting eyes of the "evil" parents. It was glorious until we dropped the box. I didn't know cereal could make so much noise. The roar seemed to last an eternity as the sweet cinnamon O's spilled down what seemed to be 5,000 hardwood steps. The silence that followed was deafening. We waited for the sound all children who've done wrong fear—heavy dad-steps.

I'm not sure why we were so offended that the punishment included picking up all the cereal. But as we sat and picked up the endless piles of cereal piece by piece, we schemed. We would escape this treacherous rule of terror. We opened the window at the back of the kitchen and slithered into the backyard. We had done it. Freedom at last! But free from what? What if we were caught? The idea that we could be in deeper trouble struck hard as we headed for the only other house we knew. Our neighbor down the street had deep window wells and we went into hiding.

I'm sure it was only a few minutes, but it seemed like hours. The reality that there was a higher power came over us, literally over us. As I peered over the edge of the galvanized metal, there they were as tall as the trees in our backyard—two polyester-clad legs attached to a very angry man with a belt. We learned that day that a father was something to be feared and not to be escaped.

Fear is not necessarily a bad thing. Fearing our father and mother protected us from our own ignorance. Parents have all kinds of rules designed to protect us. "Don't stick things in the outlet!" "Don't suck on marbles!" Rules like those make no sense to an inquisitive child. However, as children we understand that the mommy and daddy said no. Fear does serve its purpose for the young and naive.

For most parents, surviving the adolescent years is at best a calculated risk in sanity management. I remember looking my mom in the eyes. My mind was pondering these eternal questions of authority. I said, "You know,

Mom, I'm pretty sure I could knock you across the room. But, there's something inside of me that just says I better not try it." Her nodding head confirmed my unspoken fear. "You'd be scraping yourself off the asphalt, Son." Fear does serve its purpose. It protects us from our own foolish attempts to ignore authority.

However, the days come where we transition from obedience out of fear to obedience out of love. As the years passed and I watched my parents struggle through family issues, financial instability, and the everyday chaos of life, I saw firsthand how they sacrificed to take care of us. Seeing the depth of their love, I wanted to love them back.

I was developing a sense of what Jesus talked about when He said, "If you love me, you will obey what I command" (John 14:15). This was the transition that would lead me into the wonderful friendship that parents and children were meant to have. It created in me a need to love my parents in return.

I treasure my relationship with my parents now. I have the friendship with my father that I always wanted as a child, yet could never quite figure out how to get. I didn't realize it would come with the lessons of balancing fear and love. My father and I spend hours together talking and playing. Now don't get me wrong. As much as I tease him about being over the hill, a great-grandfather, mind you, there is still respect. It isn't born out of fear anymore. It is respect. Instead of saying, "I'm pretty sure I could take him, but I better not try." My heart responds, "Why would I want to hurt him? Look at all he has done for me."

The changing relationship with our parents is a wonderful picture of how our relationship with God is built. Like a child who is learning to control selfishness, we begin our relationship with God with a balance of fear and love. Without that sense of fear of the awesome power of God, we will try to push God around. We will reject His discipline and try to escape His correction.

Proverbs 9:10 is true, "The fear of the LORD is the beginning of wisdom." This is the best place to begin our relationship with God. When we are young in our faith, sometimes the fear of God's wrath is the only thing that keeps us from falling back into sin. However, God does not intend for our relationship to stay at this early stage of development. He wants us to move into a relationship of love.

As the Father has loved me, so have I loved you. Now remain in my love. If you obey my commands, you will remain in my love, just as I have obeyed my Father's commands and remain in his love. I have told you this so that my joy may be in you and that your joy may be complete. My command is this: Love each other as I have loved you. Greater love has no one than this, that he lay down his life for his friends. You are my friends if you do what I command. I no longer call you servants, because a servant does not know his master's business. Instead, I have called you friends, for everything that I learned from my Father I have made known to you. You did not choose me, but I chose you and appointed you to go and bear fruit—fruit that will last. Then the Father will give you whatever you ask in my name. This is my command: Love each other *(John 15:9-17)*.

Obedience to God was intended to be an act of love, not fear. We must grow up in our faith and that means falling in love with our Heavenly Father. We see that the Son has laid down His life for us and this causes us to say, "I wouldn't want to hurt Him!" In this transition, we have moved from servanthood to friendship. Developing a friendship with God then creates an atmosphere of love. In this development we lose the need for fear, because we are motivated out of love.

God is love. Whoever lives in love lives in God, and God in him. In this way, love is made complete among us so that we will have confidence on the day of judgment, because in this world we are like him. There is no fear in love. But perfect love drives out fear, because fear has to do with punishment. The one who fears is not made perfect in love *(1 John 4:16-18)*.

When we are spiritually young, we tend to operate under a more controlling hand of God. His rein on us is tighter, and learning the dos and don'ts is an important part of spiritual survival. We must learn the discipline of obedience.

As we mature, that obedience becomes second nature. We no longer struggle with whether or not we are going to serve God. We struggle with how to do it and what it means. Deep in our hearts there is a commitment to do what

God wants us to do. It is in this phase of our relationship that we begin moving from fear to friendship. Early in our relationship, our selfishness is prominent and the fear of punishment plays a significant role in changing our behavior. It isn't the only motivator. We do love God, and the Holy Spirit is beginning to deal with our selfishness. As we mature, we move toward a love-driven motivation for serving Him. God's goal for us is to be perfected in love where all fear is cast out and we naturally cry out to God, "Abba! Daddy!"

QUESTIONS TO CONSIDER

1. What motivates you to do what is right?

2. Who do you think initiated your relationship with God? You or God? Why?

3. What role does fear play in your relationship with God? Is this positive or negative? How would you like to see this change?

4. What role does love/friendship play in our relationship with God? When do you feel the most loving toward God? In what ways do you want your relationship with God to become more loving?

5. On a scale of 1 to 10, with 1 being fear-based and 10 being love-based, where would you mark your relationship with God right now?

6. Do you think God can trust you to care about how your actions make Him feel? Why? Why not?

7. What do you think needs to happen before you will be able to follow God because you love Him?

8. Would you classify your spiritual maturity as a child, an adolescent, or an adult? Why?

9. How has your behavior reflected your love for God?

SPIRIT

Praying the Lord's Prayer, Part 1

Learning to relate to God out of love is at the heart of Jesus' new name for God—Father.* This radical idea, that God is approachable like a loving father, astonished the people of His day. God was distant, not close. His name was unspeakable. They would never have believed they could be so close to God as to refer to Him as Father. Yet, Jesus taught us to approach God. He taught us to pray . . .

> *Our Father in heaven,*
> *hallowed be your name,*
> *your kingdom come,*
> *your will be done*
>> *on earth as it is in heaven.*
> *Give us today our daily bread.*
> *Forgive us our debts,*
>> *as we also have forgiven our debtors.*
> *And lead us not into temptation,*
> *but deliver us from the evil one* (Matthew 6:9-13).

---

*Although God is called Father in the Old Testament (see Isaiah 63:16; 64:8), the title is formal and lacks the intimate meaning Jesus gives it. His use of the Aramaic word *Abba*, or "Daddy," to speak of God further underlines the idea of closeness (see Mark 14:36).

This beautiful prayer can be used to open you to this developing friendship with our Heavenly Father. Over the next couple of weeks, the Spirit section will lead you through the Lord's Prayer as a pattern for prayer. Next week's Truth section will focus entirely on this pattern for prayer. Each day you will focus on a different part of the prayer. Toward the end of the second week you will begin praying the entire prayer. This week we will focus on the first half of the prayer. Next week, we will add the second half.

"Our Father"—He is close, not distant. He is *our* Father—we were never intended to be spiritually isolated. He loves us and wants what is best for us.

"In heaven"—We live with the realities of life on earth. While God is close, He is above all so that He can see the big picture.

"Hallowed be your name"—We are to respect and honor His name. Take a few minutes to praise God for who He is and what He has been to you.

"Your kingdom come"—Pray for God's kingdom to get larger in your circles of influence. Pray for those who need God in their lives. What is God asking you to do to advance His kingdom?

"Your will be done on earth as it is in heaven"—In heaven God's will is always done. Pray that God will help you remain obedient.

As you walk through this prayer this week, ask God to help you follow Him out of love rather than fear. As you develop your love for God, He will truly become Father to you.

SPIRITUAL JOURNEY JOURNAL

WEEK 3

Before you dive into your Spiritual Journey Journal this week, establish a place and a time for you to continue the *personal worship* you began last week. Once you've decided where, when, and how often, make sure you write this into your calendar. Remember to protect your time with God as you would any other scheduled meeting.

Begin each day this week by reading the scripture passage listed. Try to write a short breath prayer from the passage to use throughout the day. In the evening record your thoughts, insights, and any ways you found God calling you to transformation during the day. You will find between your breath prayers and your personal worship time that God will really begin challenging you and changing you.

Each day pray through the Lord's Prayer. Take as much or as little time as you need. Begin focusing on expressing love to God. Ask Him to help you follow Him out of your love for Him.

My Place for Personal Worship Is . . .

My Time(s) for Personal Worship Is (Are) . . .

Monday

Scripture: John 15:9-17

Breath Prayer: Develop a breath prayer using "Our Father."

Self-Evaluation—God's call to transformation:

Tuesday

Scripture: Proverbs 1:7

Breath Prayer: Develop a breath prayer using "in heaven."

Self-Evaluation—God's call to transformation:

Wednesday

Scripture: Proverbs 9:10-12

Breath Prayer: Develop a breath prayer using "hallowed be your name."

Self-Evaluation—God's call to transformation:

Thursday

Scripture: 1 John 4:16-18

Breath Prayer: Develop a breath prayer using "your kingdom come."

Self-Evaluation—God's call to transformation:

Friday

Scripture: Romans 8:15-16

Breath Prayer: Develop a breath prayer around the idea "your will be done on earth as it is in heaven."

Self-Evaluation—God's call to transformation:

Saturday

Scripture: Philippians 2:12-13

Prayer Time: Take the first half of the Lord's Prayer, and use the following as a guide for your prayer time.

Our Father—Take a few minutes to declare your love for God. He is Abba!

In heaven—Ask God to remind you He is above all things.

Hallowed be your name—Praise God for who He is. What names for God are especially real for you right now? (e.g., Prince of Peace, Light of the World, Lamb of God, etc.) Ask God to help you be true to the family name.

Your kingdom come—Ask God to help you be a part of advancing His kingdom. Ask God to show you faces of those He wants you to share your faith story with. Ask God to show you how He wants to use you to support your church, your Sunday School class, your pastor. Ask God to show you any way in which His kingdom is losing importance in your life, and then pray for help in changing.

Your will be done on earth as it is in heaven—Confess to God those areas where you are struggling to follow His will. Ask Him to help you submit your will to His. Commit to allow Him to lead your life without any interference.

Self-Evaluation—God's call to transformation:

Sunday

Before leaving for church, read today's scripture passage and ask God to draw near to you. Use the sections below to guide you on this Sabbath Day as you worship and spend time with God.

Scripture: 1 Peter 1:17-23

Prayer Time: Take the first half of the Lord's Prayer and use the same guide followed Saturday for your prayer time.

Insights from Sunday School/Bible Study/Small-Group Time:

Preparing for Worship:

During worship, I need You to do this in my heart . . .

As I come to worship, I need You to know . . .

Insights from Worship:

Reflecting on this Sabbath . . .

Today, God, You showed me . . .

This week I want You to do this in my heart . . .

Self-Evaluation—God's call to transformation:

FOUR

CONNECTING WITH GOD THROUGH PRAYER

TRUTH

Sixth grade was awkward enough, but I was carrying quite a bit of baby fat. I was sure that meant I was not marriage material. Melissa was the most beautiful brunette in the pool, and I was smitten to my socks. I made up my mind I wanted to go out with Melissa.

Melissa was as shy as I was fat. So getting into a conversation about dating as sixth graders was all but impossible. There was only one solution. Send a third party to do the talking for me. Her brother had the same body shape as mine. He would understand my plight. If anyone could get through to her, *he* could.

I set the plan into motion. Her brother went to deliver the good news that she was loved. A few minutes later he swam back over to me with the wonderful news: "She thinks you're fat."

I couldn't believe it. I thought this kid would fight for me. He must have known the truth all of us chubby kids knew, "It's what's on the inside that counts!"

It looked like I would have to approach the fair maiden myself. My plan was to make sure that only my head was above the water. That way she might ignore my girth.

Melissa finally said she would date me. In sixth grade, that meant holding hands during the swimming break each day at the community pool. This was the first time I realized this relationship thing was tough. I had the most wonderful treasure in town holding my hand, and I didn't know what to say. The relationship was short-lived.

Our relationship with God can feel like this. We've got a wonderful treasure and we're not sure what to say or how to say it. To make things even worse, we can't see Him. So, talking to God may seem a little ridiculous.

We are not the first to feel inadequate when it comes to talking to God. Even Jesus' disciples asked Him to teach them to pray. They didn't know how to talk to God with the same intimacy Jesus did. Jesus understood and taught His disciples to pray by doing two things. First, He taught them some basic communication skills. Second, He showed them how to pray by praying himself. In this Truth section, we are going to look at what Jesus taught the disciples about how to pray. The Spirit section will give you the chance to deepen your prayer time.

Jesus taught His disciples about prayer in Matthew 6. Read the passage and keep your Bible open to it for ready reference.

Melissa and I had a major communication problem—neither of us had a clue what to say or how to say it. That is exactly where Jesus begins with prayer. Prayer isn't for show. Just be yourself. Don't try to impress God or pretend to be something you are not. Be real with God (see vv. 5-6). God wants you to talk to Him like you would a friend. As a dear friend, He already knows your heart. But He still wants you to take the time to talk about it with Him (see vv. 7-8).

After teaching the proper attitude, Jesus taught a pattern for prayer. That doesn't mean that we are supposed to mindlessly repeat the prayer like a mantra. Each part of the prayer gives us some basic instructions on where to move in a conversation with God.

To *hallow His name* is to reverence His identity as holy. Begin with praising God for who He is. Then ask God to show you any way you might be showing disrespect to Him by what you say or do.

To pray for *His kingdom to come and His will to be done* means that you recognize Him as the one true Leader in your life. You are asking Him to fill your life and to put His plans into motion through you.

Once you have established God's place as Leader, it's time to talk about your needs. Asking God to give you *daily bread* is to invite Him to provide for your needs just like He provided for the children of Israel in the desert. Six days each week for 40 years, God provided manna (Exodus 16:10-35). This heavenly bread tasted like wafers made with honey. The people learned to depend on God each day for that day's needs. Jesus invites us to ask God for what we need each day and trust His provision without worrying for tomorrow. We are confident that He is in charge.

The next couple of sentences focus on *forgiveness and being forgiving*. We ask God to help us relate to Him and others in an attitude of grace. We confess our sin. We forgive others. We remind ourselves that we would be in serious trouble without God's help. We commit ourselves to refuse to be harsher in our judgment than God. We forgive those who have hurt us and ask God to forgive us with the same level of forgiveness we are giving others.

In the middle of this prayer for a life full of grace, Jesus reminds us to be honest about our weakness. *"Don't lead me into temptation, God."* I need God to help me deal with my weaknesses. I need to ask God to steer me clear of those places where I will face temptation. Honest confession is the key. I confess to God when I am tempted, and I ask for immediate intervention. I confess to God when I sin, and I ask God for forgiveness and help.

At the end of the prayer, after committing ourselves to lovingly and obediently following God, Jesus reminds us to pray for protection from forces aimed at our destruction: *"Deliver us from the evil one."*

Jesus organized the pattern prayer by focusing on God first and our needs second. When we see who God is, our needs seem more manageable. That includes forgiving others and overcoming temptation and evil. The prayer concludes requesting God's protection, not our own power. Evil is defeated when we are in Christ. Christ in us is more powerful than Satan and his armies.

Prayer may seem awkward at first, but we can learn good communication skills. Practice helps. We need to practice listening to what God tells us through Scripture and prayer. We need to practice making honest confession and requests. The day will come when we will move beyond sixth grade communication and move into deep friendship with God. We get to know Him and fall more and more in love with Him. And like the disciples, Jesus looks at us and says, "I no longer call you servants. . . . Instead, I have called you friends" (John 15:15). It is in prayer that we gain the deepest intimacy with God. We get to know Him and His voice. We become friends.

QUESTIONS TO CONSIDER

1. In what ways do you find it difficult to have meaningful prayer times? What distractions are most difficult for you to avoid?

2. When you think of God, does He feel like a loving father? Why or why not? If He doesn't feel like a father, how does He feel to you? What do you think needs to change in order for you to sense God as a loving and patient father?

3. How do you respond to problems that seem overwhelming? What do you want to tell God during those times? For God to be "in heaven"

means He is bigger than our problems. How would your response to difficulties change if you really believed God is bigger than the problems?

4. If you call yourself a Christian, what kind of reputation do your actions give God?

5. What are some names for God that have special significance to you because of what you have seen God do in your life? If you had to give God a special title for the way He has helped you, what title would you give Him?

6. In what ways do you resist allowing God's kingdom to come in your life? In what ways are you working to see God's kingdom become a reality in your life?

7. Where do your will and God's will conflict the most? How do you handle this battle of the wills? Is God's will done in your life "as it is in heaven"? What must happen for you to be-

come completely obedient to what you know God wants from you?

8. How difficult is it for you to trust God to provide for your needs? How important is it for you to know what is coming tomorrow?

9. Who do you need to forgive? If God were to forgive you at the same level you forgive others, would you feel confident that God would be able to forgive you?

10. What temptations are most difficult for you to resist? If you were to ask God to lead you away from temptation and deliver you from the Evil One, where would you stop going? How do you respond to the more difficult temptations in your life? How might you apply this prayer to help you overcome those temptations?

SPIRIT

Praying the Lord's Prayer, Part 2

Last week we focused on the first half of the Lord's Prayer. Today we will add the second half of the prayer to your daily spiritual journey. As you are focusing on developing a friendship with God, use the prayer as a foundation in your communication with God.

> *Our Father in heaven,*
> *hallowed be your name,*
> *your kingdom come,*
> *your will be done*
> > *on earth as it is in heaven.*
> **Give us today our daily bread.**
> **Forgive us our debts,**
> > **as we also have forgiven our debtors.**
> **And lead us not into temptation,**
> **but deliver us from the evil one** (Matthew 6:9-13).

As you pray this week, take a few moments to focus your communication with God on each of the following parts of the Lord's Prayer.

"Give us today our daily bread"—This reminds us how God provided for the children of Israel in the desert. Use this part of the prayer to help you sense your dependence. "God, teach me that You are all I need and that You provide for my needs." Ask God to help you trust Him for all your needs. Ask Him to help you follow Jesus' teaching to only focus on today's needs. Tomorrow is always in God's hands.

"Forgive us our debts"—Confess any unforgiven sin to God and ask Him to forgive you.

"As we also have forgiven our debtors"—This is a dangerous prayer. You are asking God to forgive you to the same degree you choose to forgive others. Jesus is teaching us that our own forgiveness is directly tied to the forgiveness that we extend to others. Forgive those who have harmed you.

"Lead us not into temptation"—Admit where you are most vulnerable to spiritual failure and ask God to help you. Pray for wisdom and courage to avoid sources of temptation. Ask God to protect you from yourself.

"But deliver us from the evil one"—Ask God to deliver you from Satan's attacks. No one can force you to choose to sin. Sin is always a personal decision. There are forces at work against you, but God is far stronger. Ask and receive His protection and deliverance.

As you pray the Lord's Prayer, communicate with God fully and honestly. This will help you move beyond small talk and get serious with God.

SPIRITUAL JOURNEY JOURNAL

WEEK 4

Before you dive into your Spiritual Journey Journal this week, establish a place and a time for you to continue your *personal worship*. Make plans for Sunday as you worship in *community*.

Begin each day this week by reading the scripture passage listed. Try to write a short breath prayer from the passage to use throughout the day. In the evening record your thoughts, insights, and any ways you found God calling you to transformation during the day.

Each day pray through the Lord's Prayer. Take as much or as little time as you need. Begin focusing on expressing love to God. Ask Him to help you follow Him out of your love for Him.

My Place for Personal Worship Is . . .

My Time(s) for Personal Worship Is (Are) . . .

Monday

Scripture: Matthew 6:5-6

Breath Prayer: Develop a breath prayer using "daily bread."

Self-Evaluation—God's call to transformation:

Tuesday

Scripture: Matthew 6:7-8

Breath Prayer: Develop a breath prayer using "forgive us our debts (sins)."

Self-Evaluation—God's call to transformation:

Wednesday

Scripture: Matthew 6:9

Breath Prayer: Develop a breath prayer using "as we forgive our debtors."

Self-Evaluation—God's call to transformation:

Thursday

Scripture: Matthew 6:10

Breath Prayer: Develop a breath prayer using "lead us not into temptation."

Self-Evaluation—God's call to transformation:

Friday

Scripture: Matthew 6:11

Breath Prayer: Develop a breath prayer around the idea "deliver us from the evil one."

Self-Evaluation—God's call to transformation:

Saturday

Scripture: Matthew 6:12

Prayer Time: Take the first half of the Lord's Prayer, and use the following as a guide for your prayer time.

Our Father—Take a few minutes to declare your love for God. He is Abba!

In heaven—Ask God to remind you He is above all things.

Hallowed be your name—Praise God for who He is. What names for God are especially real for you right now? (e.g., Prince of Peace, Light of the World, Lamb of God, etc.) Ask God to help you be true to the family name.

Your kingdom come—Ask God to help you be a part of advancing His kingdom. Ask God to show you faces of those He wants you to share your faith story with. Ask God to show you how He wants to use you to support your church, your Sunday School class, your pastor. Ask God to show you any way in which His kingdom is losing importance in your life, and then pray for help in changing.

Your will be done on earth as it is in heaven—Confess to God those areas where you are struggling to follow His will. Ask Him to help you submit your will to His. Commit to allow Him to lead your life without any interference.

Give us this day our daily bread—Ask God to help you learn dependence. Ask Him to help you trust His ability to provide for you even when the future seems unclear. Confess those areas where it is difficult for you to trust God to provide for your needs.

Forgive us our debts (sins)—Confess to God your sins. Be honest. Ask God to apply Jesus' death payment to your spiritual debt load.

As we forgive our debtors—Ask God to give you the ability to forgive. Ask Him to make you accountable for the amount of mercy and grace you show others today. Ask Him to keep you aware that your forgiveness is contingent on forgiving others. Ask for strength to resolve the conflicts in your life. Ask for the ability to let go of the right to hold others accountable to you for what they have done to you.

Lead us not into temptation—Ask God to give you the courage to stay away from those things that are sources of temptation in your life. Be honest with God about what those things are. Ask

God to bring an accountability partner into your life—someone who will have the right to check up on you.

Deliver us from the evil one—Ask God to protect you from Satan's schemes to attack you. Thank God that Jesus has already defeated Satan and that Jesus is living in you. Profess your allegiance to God and tell the devil to flee your life, your family, and your home.

Self-Evaluation—God's call to transformation:

Sunday

Before leaving for church, read today's scripture passage and ask God to draw near to you. Use the sections below to guide you on this Sabbath Day as you worship and spend time with God.

Scripture: Matthew 6:13

Prayer Time: Take the first half of the Lord's Prayer and use the same guide followed Saturday for your prayer time.

Insights from Sunday School/Bible Study/Small-Group Time:

Preparing for Worship:

During worship, I need You to do this in my heart . . .

As I come to worship, I need You to know . . .

Insights from Worship:

Reflecting on this Sabbath . . .

Today, God, You showed me . . .

This week I want You to do this in my heart . . .

Self-Evaluation—God's call to transformation:

FIVE

CONNECTING WITH GOD THROUGH THE BIBLE

TRUTH

It was early in our dating relationship. My future wife was walking across the campus at Olivet Nazarene University. I loved her so much that I had the deep feeling that someday I was going to change her name from Kupfersmith to Stirratt. She didn't see me come out of the student union. I yelled, "Hey, Kupfersmith!"

She turned around with a stunned glare. "Horse meat? Who are you calling horse meat?" And so, our relationship began.

Communicating is difficult, especially when you don't hear or understand exactly what was said. In a playful moment, my wife asked me a tender question. "Honey, how come you're so cute?" Wanting to express my love, I said, "Next to you, honey, anyone would look cute." I was attempting a compliment. I meant to say something like, "When someone stands next to you, your beauty radiates to them and they are improved by your beauty." It just didn't come out that way. Communicating is tough. You have to know who is talking, to whom he or she is talking, and the intent of the conversation. That is a tall order.

This is exactly the problem we face in trying to communicate with God through reading the Bible. We have a collection of documents written by different people at different times, to different people, for different reasons. That means we are trying to understand statements written in a different time, in a different situation, to a specific audience, for a specific reason. No wonder we have a difficult time understanding the conversations we read in the Bible.

As a sanguine personality, I am among that portion of the population classified as a party waiting to happen. That means I have the ability to talk to one person while looking for the next person with whom to talk. That can be irritating if you try to talk to me in a crowded room. I am easily distracted. I try to pay attention to you, really, but I have a difficult time ignoring all the activity around me. I find that I have to force myself to keep my eyes focused on the other person in the conversation.

That is the first secret for reading the Bible. To understand the book you are reading, it helps to visualize the writer. Who was he? When did he live? What was his background? What are some of the themes of his writing? You can't fully appreciate the conversation until you know who is talking.

I hate it when someone jumps into a conversation I'm having with someone else, always assuming he or she knows what we are talking about. He or she often says something that makes perfect sense to him or her but out of context in the true conversation. It is important to avoid making that mistake with the conversations in the Bible.

When we read, we are eavesdropping on a conversation already underway. This means we need to find out not only who is talking but also who was originally listening. Who are they? Where do they live? What are the problems they are trying to solve? This can help you understand why the person speaking says what he says.

Isn't this about listening to God? Yes! Then why take the time to find out about the author and his audience?

God is talking through these authors to their audience and ultimately to us. God had principles to teach the original hearers, principles that we need to learn as well. As God was revealing himself to these people through the insights of the author, God was also revealing His character to us. God's Spirit takes those truths in the original conversation and helps us apply them to our lives now. Once we hear the original conversation, God uses that to begin a conversation with us. What He said to them, He recommunicates to us in the context of our lives.

How do I learn about the author and audience of a book in the Bible? That's easier than you might think. There are tools such as Bible handbooks and commentaries that specialize in that information. Ask your pastor to recommend tools that would fit your current understanding about the Bible. Your pastor is the best resource to make sure what you find is helpful rather than confusing.

Connecting with God through the Bible is not just studying information. This is a two-way conversation. God speaks to us through the conversations in the Bible. However, we can talk to Him as well. We need to tell God how we feel about what we are learning. We need to ask Him to help us live new truth. We can even ask Him to help us deal with what we don't like about what He said.

Some people like to record their conversations with God in a journal. As they come to grips with more truth, and see their life change, they can look back over the course of their faith journey and see the path they took.

Some people prefer to use these insights from the Bible as a starting place for prayer. I talk to God and expect God to talk to me through the Bible. As I see a new insight, I stop and take the time to talk to God about it. I must be patient, attentive, and trust the still small voice of His Spirit. However, I have found it to be an amazing journey of conversation with God.

God gave us the Bible so that we can have a conversation with Him. However, like any communication, you will need to focus on the conversation. If you invest yourself in listening well, you will hear and be able to respond to the message God has for you. It will lead you on a tremendous adventure in loving God and living for Him.

QUESTIONS TO CONSIDER

1. Think about your relationships right now. How important is communication to the health of those relationships? How do you make sure you are taking time to communicate in these relationships? How can that be applied to your growing relationship with God?

2. How do you converse with God now? Do you consider these one-way or two-way conversations? Who does most of the talking?

3. Have you ever felt like you have heard God trying to tell you something? What were some of the questions you had? What parts of this were difficult?

4. How much time do you spend trying to learn what is in the Bible? Do you feel like this is adequate? What can you do this week to begin investigating one of the books of the Bible? Who can you ask for help? Are there any groups meeting in your church who study the Bible on a consistent basis? Who do you need to talk to in order to join one of those groups?

SPIRIT

Studying God's Word Through the Sermon

This week we've explored the idea that the Bible is a conversation between God and us. One way we can begin exploring the Bible is to use the pastor's sermon as a source of Bible study. This is a special time during the week when God can use the Bible, His Spirit, and the anointing of the pastor to communicate the Word to us.

Another benefit of using a sermon as the source of Bible study is that pastors often give examples of how we can apply the original conversation between the author and audience to our situation. The pastor has done much of the work for us. We just have to actively listen and learn. As we listen to how the pastor interpreted the conversation, we learn what is appropriate and inappropriate in Bible study.

This week be sure to listen and take notes on your pastor's sermon. Listen for some of the primary Bible study questions mentioned in this week's devotional. Who is the author of the book? Who was the first audience receiving this message? What problem did they have? How did they apply the truth to their situation? How can we apply those principles to our lives? You might even want to have lunch with your pastor during the week to discuss the insights you gained and ask for feedback.

SPIRITUAL JOURNEY JOURNAL

WEEK 5

Before you dive into your Spiritual Journey Journal this week, establish a place and a time for you to continue your *personal worship*. Make plans for Sunday as you worship in *community*.

Begin each day this week by reading the scripture passage listed. Try to write a short breath prayer from the passage to use throughout the day. In the evening record your thoughts, insights, and any ways you found God calling you to transformation during the day.

If you found the Lord's Prayer to be a helpful starting place for prayer, continue using that model each day this week. Or if you haven't practiced the praying the Scriptures technique described earlier, try using it to take your Bible reading into your prayer time.

My Place for Personal Worship Is . . .

My Time(s) for Personal Worship Is (Are) . . .

Monday

Scripture: Psalm 119:9-16
Breath Prayer:

Self-Evaluation—God's call to transformation:

Tuesday

Scripture: 2 Timothy 3:12-16
Breath Prayer:

Self-Evaluation—God's call to transformation:

Wednesday

Scripture: John 15:14-15
Breath Prayer:

Self-Evaluation—God's call to transformation:

Thursday

Scripture: Acts 2:42-47

Breath Prayer:

Self-Evaluation—God's call to transformation:

Friday

Scripture: Hebrews 12:1-3

Breath Prayer:

Self-Evaluation—God's call to transformation:

Saturday

Scripture: Matthew 4:1-11

Breath Prayer:

Self-Evaluation—God's call to transformation:

Sunday

Before leaving for church, read today's scripture passage, write out and pray your breath prayer, and ask God to draw near to you. Use the sections below to guide you on this Sabbath Day as you worship and spend time with God.

Scripture: Psalm 111:1-2

Breath Prayer:

Insights from Sunday School/Bible Study/Small-Group Time:

Preparing for Worship:

During worship, I need You to do this in my heart . . .

As I come to worship, I need You to know . . .

Insights from Worship:

Reflecting on this Sabbath . . .

Today, God, You showed me . . .

This week I want You to do this in my heart . . .

Self-Evaluation—God's call to transformation:

SIX

CONNECTING WITH GOD THROUGH WORSHIP

TRUTH

Falling in love is never as difficult as staying in love. This is true in our human relationships as well as our relationship with God. I am constantly dealing with older men who are pessimistic about the joy of marriage. Yes, they love their spouse. Yet, for all their talk of devotion, they have fallen out of love. They've lost the passion of love. Their relationship functions as a matter of habit. It shouldn't be. Most of these men would be the first to say, "I wish it were different." Somewhere along the way, we all face the temptation to let the spark go out of our relationships. Routine sets in and we find that we aren't even trying to keep the romance alive.

Many books tell how to rekindle the flame of love in marriage. I want to talk about how to fan the flame of love in your relationship with God. How do we keep our passion for God alive?

Without a doubt, we lose the passion in any relationship when we quit expressing our love in tangible ways. We have an incredible ability to lose the passion when we don't act passionately. So, how do you express love to God? Jesus said obedience to Him is the *result* of love. "If you love me, you will obey me." The question is, How do we keep the love strong so that the passion doesn't die? The answer is one word: *worship!*

Think about it. When we first fall in love with someone there is a kind of all-consuming focus on that person that fans the flame of passion. We can't do anything but think about that person. As this singular focus fades, we look at those who still have the passion with a bit of condescension. We watch newlyweds buy a car with a bench seat so they can sit next to each other. We cry out, "It'll pass!" The truth is that we are jealous and long to rekindle that same kind of passion.

How do we lose it? Somewhere along the way, we quit paying attention to all the things that are right about our spouse and started focusing on the things that are less than perfect. Now, it isn't that those imperfections suddenly showed up. As our adoration lost its focus, our disappointment with our spouse increased. The secret for staying in passionate love is to *choose* to adore.

This is true in keeping our passion for God alive. Worshiping God is the way we choose to adore Him. We choose to express our adoration for all that He is by focusing on the perfection of His character, compassion, and love. This keeps our passion bright and strong.

When I worship I choose to express my passionate love for God regardless of how perfect or imperfect I believe life is. God is perfect and I choose to love Him and to worship Him. Yes, I am tempted to consider the things in my life that haven't turned out as I planned. I might even be tempted to treat God like some men treat their wives, "The problems in my life are God's fault." We might even be tempted to say of those young in their love for God, "They are so idealistic. They will learn!" We can avoid that pessimistic temptation. We can choose blissful adoration: worship.

So, how do you worship God? There are two primary forms of worship. There is the kind of worship that happens between just God and an individual. That is personal worship. In the quietness of my home or in the car on the way to work, I worship Him. It might be with music playing or in the quietness of the ride. Regardless of how I do it, I focus on adoring Him. I reflect on what has happened in the past few days, and I thank God for all He's done. I think about the days to come, and I thank God that I know He is moving into these uncertain days with me. I place my thoughts on all that is good about God and what that means for my life. I thank Him, worship Him, and love Him.

This is so important. To neglect this area is like spending day after day with my spouse without ever expressing any kind of love to her. Refusing to spend time with God is like refusing to show love to your spouse. It is easy to get sloppy in your relationship skills. It takes effort to keep the passion alive. Your love for God stays strong when you focus on adoring Him.

The second kind of worship happens when we come together to worship God. This is corporate worship. It happens at places such as concerts, camps, worship services, and other special events. Just like a family has regular times of expressing their love for each other at Thanksgiving, Christmas, birthdays, and anniversaries, the family of God comes together to celebrate. God has made us a family!

God loves us all so much that we are no longer alone. We sing songs, watch dramas, read the Bible, pray, laugh, and cry. It is all a time of adoring the Father who has made us family. As our voices rise, the house of God is filled with the joyful sound of the family. Every week is an opportunity to join our worship with the worship of others in the family of God. Together we lift up an offering of love to God.

How does all of this help us connect in a friendship with God? Something happens to us in the middle of this kind of expression of our love for God. Our awareness of His presence is elevated, and He transforms us bit by bit as we stay in His presence. Our character is changed to look like His as we spend time in this place of worship, this place of focused adoration. It is more mystical than rational. Somehow, by spending time expressing love for God, He is able to transform our inner being in ways that couldn't be done in any other way. Adoration works its way deep into the deepest parts of our character. Its heat melts us and re-molds us into people who look more and more like our Heavenly Father. God uses this time to connect with us spiritually. It is in these times that we move beyond knowing *about* God to truly *knowing* God. We adore Him more and we love Him more. This is the power of worship.

QUESTIONS TO CONSIDER

1. What difficulties have you had trying to spend time worshiping God away from church? What have you learned that might help you? When could you set aside some time for personal worship?

2. List four or five things God has been doing in your life in the past weeks. Take a minute to thank God for each one regardless of whether these things have been pleasant or painful.

3. What has your attitude been as you came into the worship service in the last few weeks? How can you adjust your attitude so that you can enjoy the idea of worshiping together? How can you prepare your heart and mind to spend the worship service adoring God?

4. On a scale of 1 to 10, how passionate is your adoration of God? How much are you focusing on the good things about what God is doing in your life? How distracted by the circumstances

of your life have you been? How can you stop and refocus your attention on God?

5. Take a minute and write a simple love letter to God. Ask Him to help you focus your attention on loving Him. Ask Him to help you spend time daily adoring Him. Ask Him to help you come into corporate worship with an expectation of spending time in His presence.

SPIRIT

Expressing Love Through Music

Whether or not you are musical, music touches the soul. God gave us music to express some of our deepest thoughts and emotions. One entire book of the Bible is nothing but songs: the Book of Psalms.

You may or may not enjoy singing. You might like hard rock or you might be a country and western fan. Regardless of what style of music you enjoy, it can become a source of worship. It isn't too difficult to find music written by Christians in almost any musical style. A trip to your local Christian bookstore is a good place to start.

There are several ways you can use music in personal and corporate worship. Let's begin with your personal worship. You might want to get some CDs or tapes and keep them where you normally have your personal worship. That might be in a special room in your house, in the car, or in a portable player. Wherever you worship, have music that you enjoy and that praises God. If you like to sing, sing along. If you enjoy just listening, then use the music to help you focus on God. Some people enjoy reading the songs in a hymnal. The words are powerful and can help draw you close to God.

Most cannot choose the kind of music used in corporate worship unless they are on the team that plans music. However, you can politely make suggestions to your pastor or worship leaders. Whatever the style of music may be in church, focus on expressing love to God as a family. Sometimes we listen to music that isn't our personal favorite because someone we love enjoys it. If you prefer not to sing, let the words pass through your mind. Use the words to express adoration to God. If someone else is singing, let their words of praise become yours. Listen prayerfully and join in their adoration of God. This is an ideal time for simple sentence prayers.

"Yes, Lord."

"Let this be true in my life, God."

"You are worthy of worship, Lord!"

"Amen!"

The point is to let God take the music and touch you. Then in the middle of your adoration, your heart will be drawn to God.

Music can be a powerful tool for worship. Take a trip to a Christian bookstore. Ask for help finding music that fits your preferences. Invest a little in a CD or two and ask God to use the music to draw you close to Him.

SPIRITUAL JOURNEY JOURNAL

WEEK 6

Before you dive into your Spiritual Journey Journal this week, establish a place and a time for you to continue your *personal worship*. Try to find some music that will help you worship. Make plans for Sunday as you worship in *community*.

Begin each day this week by reading the scripture passage listed. Try to write a short breath prayer from the passage to use throughout the day. In the evening record your thoughts, insights, and any ways you found God calling you to transformation during the day.

If you found the Lord's Prayer to be a helpful starting place for prayer, continue using that model each day this week. Or if you haven't practiced the praying the Scriptures technique described earlier, try using it to take your Bible reading into your prayer time.

My Place for Personal Worship Is . . .

My Time(s) for Personal Worship Is (Are) . . .

Monday

Scripture: 2 Corinthians 3:12-18

Breath Prayer:

Self-Evaluation—God's call to transformation:

Tuesday

Scripture: 1 John 4:13-16
Breath Prayer:

Self-Evaluation—God's call to transformation:

Wednesday

Scripture: John 4:1-26
Breath Prayer:

Self-Evaluation—God's call to transformation:

Thursday

Scripture: Ephesians 5:15-20
Breath Prayer:

Self-Evaluation—God's call to transformation:

Friday

Scripture: Psalm 27:4
Breath Prayer:

Self-Evaluation—God's call to transformation:

Saturday

Scripture: Nehemiah 9:5-6
Breath Prayer:

Self-Evaluation—God's call to transformation:

Sunday

Before leaving for church, read today's scripture passage, write out and pray your breath prayer, and ask God to draw near to you. Use the sections below to guide you on this Sabbath Day as you worship and spend time with God.

Scripture: Psalm 122:1

Breath Prayer:

Insights from Sunday School/Bible Study/Small-Group Time:

Preparing for Worship:

During worship, I need You to do this in my heart . . .

As I come to worship, I need You to know . . .

Insights from Worship:

Reflecting on this Sabbath . . .

Today, God, You showed me . . .

This week I want You to do this in my heart . . .

Self-Evaluation—God's call to transformation:

SEVEN

DEVELOPING SENSITIVITY TO THE SPIRIT

TRUTH

People have always looked for the key ingredients to keep their love alive. It is tough to keep a relationship with another person alive. It isn't any easier with God. How do you develop a relationship with an invisible Creator who speaks to us through His Spirit and the Word?

Because I love God, I want to serve and obey Him. When He talks, I *want* to listen and obey. When He shows me I am doing something wrong, I don't run and hide. I want to confess and turn away from the sin. When God speaks, I listen. When He checks me, I stop. When He calls me, I follow. I respond to His leadership. If we are going to keep this friendship we've been building, then we must maintain our sensitivity to the Spirit.

We shouldn't take our sensitivity to the Spirit for granted. There is an ongoing battle for the control of our lives. If the Spirit doesn't lead us, we will become uncontrollably selfish. When we are controlled by our flesh, our rebellion to God is so complete we don't even want to listen to God, let alone obey Him. Sensitivity to the Spirit, the willingness to listen and obey, allows us to keep our love for God deep and rich. Paul explains our need in the Book of Ephesians.

In chapter 3, verses 14-19 Paul gives his prayer for the Ephesians. The prayer is appropriate for us today. He prays that Christ would dwell in their hearts through faith. We recognize our sin, confess it to God, and ask God to lead our lives. God then graciously forgives us and makes us His children. Our loving relationship with God is new and exciting. It seems like nothing could be more real or full of joy.

It doesn't take too long, however, before we come face-to-face with an inner battle between what we want and what God wants. It isn't long before we identify with Paul, who found that there were two laws at work within him—one wanted what is right and the other one wanted what is wrong (see Romans 7). Paul gives us this command, "Therefore do not let sin reign in your mortal body so that you obey its evil desires" (6:12). This battle against evil desires is a battle for control. It is the same battle that Adam and Eve faced in the garden. Did they do what they wanted or what God commanded? Who controls what I think and do, the Spirit or me? Paul says:

> If our minds are ruled by our desires, we will die. But if our minds are ruled by the Spirit, we will have life and peace. Our desires fight against God, because they do not and cannot obey God's laws. If we follow our desires, we cannot please God (8:6-8, CEV).

Paul offers a continuation of his prayer in Ephesians:

> And I pray that you, being rooted and established in love, may have power, together with all the saints, to grasp how wide and long and high and deep is the love of Christ, and to know this love that surpasses knowledge—that you may be filled to the measure of all the fullness of God *(3:17-19)*.

Paul has good news for us in this struggle. The way to win is to avoid dividing our love between what God wants and what we want. We can be filled with the Spirit of God. He gives us a full and complete love for God.

Paul calls us to that moment in our relationship with God where He breaks through our selfishness and purifies our love for Him. That relationship of love must be nurtured. So later in Ephesians, Paul calls us to be continually filled with the Spirit. This allows us to fulfill the call to imitate God.

Ephesians 5 begins, "Be imitators of God, therefore, as dearly loved children" (v. 1). Paul goes on to tell how we can be imitators of God. In the list to follow he says, "Be very careful, then, how you live—not as unwise but as wise" (v. 15). Why? He already told us in 4:17-19. When we don't watch how we live, it destroys our sensitivity to the Spirit. Our flesh takes over our thinking and we shut God out of His place of leadership.

If you want to stay sensitive to the Spirit's leading in your life, you must be careful not to give your natural wants room to control you. Be careful how you live. There is nothing wrong with wants as long as we allow God to control them. The question is, How do I keep God in control? The answer brings us back to Paul's command to be filled with the Spirit.

> Do not get drunk on wine, which leads to debauchery. Instead, be [continually] filled with the Spirit. Speak to one another with psalms, hymns and spiritual songs. Sing and make music in your heart to the Lord, always giving thanks to God the Father for everything, in the name of our Lord Jesus Christ. Submit to one another out of reverence for Christ *(Ephesians 5:18-21).*

What is the crucial command? "Be [continually] filled with the Spirit" (v. 18). Why? The issue is control. Be careful of things like drunkenness because they rob you of your ability to control yourself. God's control comes through a continual filling of the Spirit.

It is important that Paul places this continued filling with the Spirit in the context of being with other believers. The Spirit helps us strengthen one another. Spiritual gifts are given to help build up the church (see 1 Corinthians 12). Paul defines the attitude believers have as they journey together. "Always giving thanks to God the Father for everything, in the name of our Lord Jesus Christ" (Ephesians 5:20). This attitude of gratitude in your spiritual journey is another characteristic of the life that is continually Spirit-filled. Thankfulness strengthens the Spirit's reign in our lives.

Paul shows us that our relationships also affect our sensitivity to the Spirit. We are called to imitate Christ by serving each other, to "submit to one another out of reverence for Christ" (v. 21). By doing these things, and being open to the Spirit, we allow Him to continually fill us with His presence and leadership.

There is one more insight Paul gives us about how to maintain this sensitivity to the Spirit of God. Paul says:

> It was he who gave some to be apostles, some to be prophets, some to be evangelists, and some to be pastors and teachers, to prepare God's people for works of service, so that the body of Christ may be built up until we all reach unity in the faith and in the knowledge of the Son of God and become mature, attaining to the whole measure of the fullness of Christ *(4:11-13)*.

As I am discipled and trained for ministry, and I use my spiritual gifts in ministry, I mature. One result of that maturity is unity with other believers. One sign that the fullness of Christ is in me is that I have a spiritual maturity that allows me to get along with others. As God's deeper love is unleashed, I mature in unity with other believers and in the use of my spiritual gifts. His leadership over my choices increases and so does my sensitivity and willingness to obey His Spirit.

QUESTIONS TO CONSIDER

1. If sensitivity to the Spirit is the willingness to obey and follow God's will, how would you rate your sensitivity on a scale of 1 to 10? How do you feel about your rating?

2. Have you ever felt like your love for God could go deeper? If you could do it, how would you improve your love for God? What would change about the way you relate to God?

3. Take a look at the list of things that Paul says help continually fill us with the Spirit. Where do you need to improve your continual filling? What can you do this week to begin improving?

4. Have you ever felt especially close to God as you were helping someone else? What was the situation? How does this help you understand Paul's statement that these things help us attain "the whole measure of the fullness of Christ" (Ephesians 4:13)?

Take a moment to pray. Ask God to help you stay sensitive to the Spirit's leadership. Be honest about the areas where your natural desires fight His control. Ask God to help you grow in your love.

SPIRIT

Tithing—Ending My Slavery to Money

Nothing competes with God's leadership in our lives more than our faith in money. Jesus focused on the problem issue in Matthew 6:24 when He said, "You cannot serve both God and Money."

What did Jesus mean? Jesus gives us a clue in chapter 23. Jesus accused the Pharisees of not caring about people. They were following some laws, like tithing (giving the first 10 percent of their income to God), but they weren't following the intent behind laws—to show love to God and others. Jesus told them they should not only tithe but also show mercy. Jesus was saying that when we love God, we want to follow *all* of His commands.

Money was the only thing Jesus ever listed as something in direct competition for our love for God. Tithing doesn't prove you love God. However, tithing is a spiritual discipline that keeps our love for God pure. He commanded us to give 10 percent of our income as an offering. The question isn't how much I have. The question is, Who owns all I have? If it is all God's stuff, then I will do with it as He commands.

Malachi 3:8 asks, "Will a man rob God?" It is a rhetorical question. Malachi calls God's people to quit robbing Him by their refusal to tithe "and see if I will not throw open the floodgates of heaven and pour out so much blessing that you will not have room enough for it" (v. 10).

When we tithe, we are on our way to managing one of the major competitors to our love for God: money. This week, set aside 10 percent of your income to give to God. Ask your pastor for tithe envelopes and for prayer as you obediently take this step of faith. If you are like most, you will be amazed at how far the 90 percent goes when you put God first and heaven's floodgates open.

SPIRITUAL JOURNEY JOURNAL

WEEK 7

Before you dive into your Spiritual Journey Journal this week, establish a place and a time for you to continue your *personal worship*. Try to find some music that will help you worship. Make plans for Sunday as you worship in *community*.

Begin each day this week by reading the scripture passage listed. Try to write a short breath prayer from the passage to use throughout the day. In the evening record your thoughts, insights, and any ways you found God calling you to transformation during the day.

If you found the Lord's Prayer to be a helpful starting place for prayer, continue using that model each day this week. Or if you haven't practiced the praying the Scriptures technique described earlier, try using it to take your Bible reading into your prayer time.

My Place for Personal Worship Is . . .

My Time(s) for Personal Worship Is (Are) . . .

Monday

Scripture: Ephesians 3:14-19
Breath Prayer:

Self-Evaluation—God's call to transformation:

Tuesday

Scripture: Ephesians 4:11-13
Breath Prayer:

Self-Evaluation—God's call to transformation:

Wednesday

Scripture: Ephesians 4:17—5:21
Breath Prayer:

Self-Evaluation—God's call to transformation:

Thursday

Scripture: Romans 7:21-25
Breath Prayer:

Self-Evaluation—God's call to transformation:

Friday

Scripture: Romans 8:5-8
Breath Prayer:

Self-Evaluation—God's call to transformation:

Saturday

Scripture: Malachi 3:6-17
Breath Prayer:

Self-Evaluation—God's call to transformation:

Sunday

Before leaving for church, read today's scripture passage, write out and pray your breath prayer, and ask God to draw near to you. Use the sections below to guide you on this Sabbath Day as you worship and spend time with God.

Scripture: Malachi 4:1-5

Breath Prayer:

God's tithe (my income this week x 10 percent): $_____

God, I trust You more than money and things. I present Your tithe as an act of worship.

Insights from Sunday School/Bible Study/Small-Group Time:

Preparing for Worship:

During worship, I need You to do this in my heart . . .

As I come to worship, I need You to know . . .

Insights from Worship:

Reflecting on this Sabbath . . .

Today, God, You showed me . . .

This week I want You to do this in my heart . . .

Self-Evaluation—God's call to transformation:

RESTORING HIS IMAGE, PART I

EIGHT

POOR IN SPIRIT

TRUTH

We had taken 15 teenagers to Chicago for the weekend. It takes some kind of arrogance to believe a youth pastor can keep 15 teenagers together and safe in downtown Chicago. Crossing the street in our small rural town was as simple as waiting for the three cars on the street to pass. Downtown Chicago operated on a completely different strategy. I call it herd strategy. The light turns and a mass of people jump into the street. As long as you're in the herd you're safe.

We had gathered the teenagers around us like the beginning of the running of the bulls. "Stay together and stay up!" was the cry. The light changed and the rush began. Our small town hearts pounded as we struggled through the rushing current of people. We were almost to the other side of the intersection when I began to hear the piercing sound of horns blowing in the intersection. I glanced back over my shoulder and terror hit. There stood Andy in the middle of the intersection.

In the chaos of the moment, I had forgotten that he was hindered by a new pair of crutches. He had gotten halfway into the intersection and had fallen behind. Deciding it would be best if he turned around and waited for the next light, Andy was now caught in the middle of irritated Chicago drivers. The light had changed and there he stood, road pizza waiting to happen. I rushed back into the intersection to pull him to safety. My prideful anger was well justified. "You need to stay close to me down here. You're going to get killed!"

After gorging ourselves on pizza, we headed back to the streets carrying a box full of leftovers. As we turned the corner we saw a smelly vagrant wearing torn clothes sleeping on the sidewalk. A piece of cardboard functioned as his bed.

It was in those moments that all my bravado about knowing the city was shattered by the *reality*. The tightness of our stomachs filled with pizza convicted us as we looked into the face of poverty. He wouldn't look us in the eye, but every teen on that street focused on him. As we passed within inches of his feet, the teens and adults fell silent. The situation was a living picture of Jesus' words, "Whatever you did for one of the least of these brothers of mine, you did for me" (Matthew 25:40). We were in one of those God moments.

We were only a few feet past the man when one of the teens turned and asked with a kind of honest desperation I hadn't heard from them before, "Isn't there anything we can do?" Suddenly I felt very poor. Who was I? I sure didn't have a way to explain the complexity of the situation to this idealistic teenager. I was crying out to God, "What can *we* do?"

Then it was like an angel tugged on the pizza box and I stopped. I turned around and headed back. I was sure this man would be offended by this generosity. But, what else could I do? I laid the box at the man's feet, and I had never been more humbled in my life. All I could give him was a few slices of pizza, and I knew it wasn't enough. The teens knew it too. But somehow in the middle of that experience God gave us all a chance to come face-to-face with our poverty before Him. We couldn't change these things. Only He could. That meant we had to call on Him for help to know what to do and how to do it.

It is in moments like this that we learn what Jesus meant by "Blessed are the poor in spirit" (Matthew 5:3). There is freshness to life, a new vitality, that comes through the abandonment of the kind of pride that says, "I know what to do. I have the answers. I have the things that I need." We learn God blesses those who know they are poor. Poverty isn't the blessing. It is the attitude of recognizing our absolute dependence on God that brings us into a new character.

What is this poverty in spirit that Jesus says brings the blessings of inheriting the Kingdom? It begins with the complete belief that we are empty-handed before God. We are like the man on the sidewalk. We have nothing to call our own and nothing to fall back on. We are exposed to the elements of life and are at God's mercy for survival. It means we recognize that all we have cannot save us or protect us. God alone is our resource, and He alone is our protection. We refuse to be impressed by our knowledge or abilities. We refuse to play the game of comparisons. "I'm better than that person because . . ." We are all poverty-stricken before God. We bring nothing to the table to bargain with. We are completely dependent on God's grace for our survival.

In this humility, we learn the true character of God. He saves those who cry out to Him (2 Samuel 22:26-30). When we seek God first, He is faithful to meet our needs. In fact, turning to God instead of trying to get stuff is what distinguishes a follower of Christ from a pagan (Matthew 6:25-34). We must learn that the poor don't have anyone to turn to other than God himself. They are desperately dependent on God. There is no bank account to trust. There isn't a storehouse to open. The poor understand Jesus' prayer, "Give us each day our *daily* bread" (Luke 11:3, emphasis added). God is faithful to the humble, and so they are blessed.

Times of difficulty reveal our true attitude, whether poverty or arrogance. We turn to the things we truly trust for help when we are desperate. I think this is why James says:

> Blessed is the man who perseveres under trial, because when he has stood the test, he will receive the crown of life that God has promised to those who love him *(James 1:12)*.

The brother in humble circumstances is proud because God is his Source (v. 9). He turns to God for help instead of other things. God is generous. The rich man takes pride because he is in a low position. The things in his life don't protect him. His attitude must be one of poverty (v. 10). The truly wise rich man says, "Regardless of all the things I have, I am only safe because of God's protection." He turns to God for help instead of trusting in his possessions.

James is clear on this issue. Being poor in spirit is about how you see your security. Whether you are poor or rich, you know that every good and perfect gift comes from God himself. We are absolutely dependent on God for all of life. Our salvation is a gift of grace. Our safety isn't provided by our education or bank accounts. We are bankrupt before God. And in this place of poverty, we are blessed because God is faithful to the humble.

It is important to remember that Jesus places this humility at the very front of His description of those who are blessed in the kingdom of God. God will bless us because we are dependent on Him for all we are.

QUESTIONS TO CONSIDER

1. What things do you tend to count on for your security? How confident are you that those sources of protection are reliable?

2. Have you ever experienced true poverty? If yes, how did that affect how you responded to God? If no, how do you think you would feel about God if you lost everything you own?

3. James says that we should consider trials pure joy because it forms our character through perseverance (James 1:2-3). Have you ever experienced what he is talking about? How did you grow in your dependence on God during those times? What was most difficult?

4. Write down the top three to five priorities of your life right now. What are you doing to stay on track with those priorities?

   My priorities   *What I'm doing to get there*

5. Where does God's will fit into those priorities? Are the ways you are seeking to fulfill those priorities reinforcing your dependence on God or weakening your dependence on God?

6. What can you do this week to reinforce an attitude of absolute dependence on God? When will you do it? Who will you ask to keep you accountable to move in this direction?

What will I do?

When will I do this?

Who will I ask to keep me accountable to this?

SPIRIT

The Hand: Simple Steps for Prayer

Prayer is one of the most rewarding things you can do to connect with God. However, for many people, prayer can be frustrating. Some people find it helpful to use this simple prayer help. Each finger of your hand represents a different part of prayer. Simply pray through the following stages using your fingers as a reminder.

PRAISE

Praise—I begin prayer offering praise to God. I begin by applauding Him for all that He is.

THANKS

Thanksgiving— I continue by thanking God for the blessings He has brought into my life. I also thank Him for difficulties and the perseverance they will bring. I practice the admonition to give thanks in all circumstances.

Confession—Once I have entered into the worship of prayer through praise and thanksgiving, I need to make sure everything is OK between God and me. I need to confess any sin that has crept into my life. I need to ask for God's forgiveness and promise my obedience as He helps me overcome temptation. I

CONFESS

need to spend some time being honest with God about the areas I am most tempted and ask God for help.

REQUESTS

Requests—Now I am ready to bring my requests to God. What issues are you facing? How do you need God to intervene? How do you need God to help you and your family?

Intercession—Intercession is praying for others. Pray for your friends, coworkers, neighbors, parents of your children's friends, leaders in your community, and your church. Pray for those you know need to know Christ. Pray for your pastor and Sunday School teacher. Just look around and you'll see people who need you to pray for them.

INTERCESSION

SPIRITUAL JOURNEY JOURNAL

WEEK 8

Before you dive into your Spiritual Journey Journal this week, establish a place and a time for you to continue your *personal worship*. Make plans for Sunday as you worship in *community*.

Begin each day this week by reading the scripture passage listed. Try to write a short breath prayer from the passage to use throughout the day. In the evening record your thoughts, insights, and any ways you found God calling you to transformation during the day.

As you pray this week, try using the hand as a model for prayer. If the Lord's Prayer is more helpful for you, use it. Feel free to experiment with what works best for you.

My Place for Personal Worship Is . . .

My Time(s) for Personal Worship Is (Are) . . .

Monday

Scripture: Matthew 5:1-12 (focus on v. 3)
Breath Prayer:

Self-Evaluation—God's call to transformation:

Tuesday

Scripture: Luke 6:20-23 (focus on v. 20)
Breath Prayer:

Self-Evaluation—God's call to transformation:

Wednesday

Scripture: Matthew 6:25-34

Breath Prayer:

Self-Evaluation—God's call to transformation:

Thursday

Scripture: 2 Samuel 22:26-30

Breath Prayer:

Self-Evaluation—God's call to transformation:

Friday

Scripture: Isaiah 29:17-19

Breath Prayer:

Self-Evaluation—God's call to transformation:

Saturday

Scripture: James 1:2-16

Breath Prayer:

Self-Evaluation—God's call to transformation:

Sunday

Before leaving for church, read today's scripture passage, write out and pray your breath prayer, and ask God to draw near to you. Use the sections below to guide you on this Sabbath Day as you worship and spend time with God.

Scripture: Psalm 25:9-10

Breath Prayer:

God's tithe (my income this week x 10 percent): $_____
God, I trust You more than money and things. I present Your tithe as an act of worship.

Insights from Sunday School/Bible Study/Small-Group Time:

Preparing for Worship:
During worship, I need You to do this in my heart . . .

As I come to worship, I need You to know . . .

Insights from Worship:

Reflecting on this Sabbath . . .
Today, God, You showed me . . .

This week I want You to do this in my heart . . .

Self-Evaluation—God's call to transformation:

NINE

MOURNING

TRUTH

Grandpa Joe was great. He was a short, pudgy, bald man. Everything about him screamed Grandpa. We used to love to climb on his lap and kiss his bald head. I was very young, but I remember those times vividly. He and Grandma lived in the hills of Missouri. Going to Grandpa's was the highlight of the summer. This year would be even better.

Mom and Dad were taking my two older brothers with them to a business convention in another part of the country. My younger brother and I wouldn't be going. But we didn't care. This was our fishing-with-Grandpa week!

My brother and I were in heaven as Grandpa drove the boat to the island in the middle of the river. We dug our own worms and headed for the adventure of the open water. My pole bent, the line wheezed out of the reel, and I screamed, "What do I do?"

Grandpa laughed and shouted, "Reel him in!" I caught an eel. It was disgusting, but I loved it. Grandpa caught a catfish or two and my little brother caught another eel. As far as grandpa-style fun goes, it couldn't get any better.

We finished the day watching Grandpa teach us the best technique for cleaning a catfish, and we were convinced he was the best grandpa in the whole world. In those few days, our love for our Grandpa Joe deepened more than it had in our seven or eight short years of life. We *loved* Grandpa.

Fourth grade began that year, and the memories of our time in Missouri became embellished as months passed. I remember my mother talking about Grandpa's health that fall. However, a fourth grader doesn't understand the implications of such things.

It was early before school and I can still see my mother's face turn pale as she answered the phone. I knew Grandpa was in the hospital. Mom had just been down to see him. However, I didn't know things were this serious. As my mother said the words, "Oh no, Mom, not Dad" and broke into tears, something tore inside of my heart. It couldn't be! Immediately the anger broke through and I began to cry uncontrollably. This wasn't right! It couldn't be. I love him. Deep inside I felt the awful reality that this wasn't supposed to be. Yet it had happened. For the first time in my short life, I mourned, deeply and painfully.

So how can Jesus be so insensitive as to claim, "Blessed are those who mourn, for they will be comforted" (Matthew 5:4). How can this have anything to do with restoring God's image in us? What could this kind of pain and sorrow have to do with finding blessing? Everything in us understands that death and sorrow are not good things. They are not to be celebrated. They are a violation of what we naturally understand should be. We were created for eternal life, not death. This just isn't right. And yet, Jesus says it clearly. You are blessed when you mourn, because you will be comforted. What does He mean and what does this have to do with restoring God's image in me?

God created us to have a relationship with Him where our character reflects His character. We were created to look like our Heavenly Father in our character. But sin has damaged that. In Adam's sin, God experienced the death of His beloved sons and daughters. That is why in Genesis 6, God grieves that He has placed man on the earth. Out of His grief He reveals a plan to restore the creation. Noah will be a fresh start. This foreshadowed the role that Jesus would play. He is the final fresh start, the answer to God's mourning over the moral and spiritual death of His children. Perhaps this is the kind of mourning Jesus talks about. "Blessed are you when you mourn over death sin brought to creation. Blessed are you when sin causes you to hurt inside because you know how deeply it hurts God. Blessed are you because God has provided a way for you to be comforted. His name is Jesus!"

Jesus calls us to a realistic approach to the world's sin. We are not to ignore it. Instead we allow it to break our hearts. The sin that infects our homes, communities, and world should cause us to mourn deeply. God's beloved creation is dead in sin. That should cause us pain. The effect of sin on humanity should cause us to weep.

And yet, death should cause us to cry out to God for help through Jesus. He is the answer to the mourning. He is the promised blessedness, the One who brings comfort to those who face death. His death on the Cross and resurrection from the grave are the source that God will use to comfort those who mourn. Spiritual death is over-come through Jesus' death. He made our redemption, rec-onciliation, and restoration possible.

Physical death is overcome through Jesus' resurrec-tion. His resurrection is proof that God will raise us from death as well (Romans 8:11). Those who mourn are now blessed because their mourning causes them to turn to the only source of hope. That source of hope is Jesus, the res-urrection and the life.

We saw this part of Jesus' character when Lazarus died. Jesus waited until Lazarus died before arriving at the family home. Jesus proclaimed, "I am the resurrection and the life" (John 11:25). He went to the tomb and wept. His friend had died. This reality broke Jesus' heart. In Christ, we see how God feels about death. Jesus stands and calls Lazarus out. Lazarus is alive. Mourning turns to blessedness.

Jesus calls us to mourn. We are to be distraught over the reality that sin is destroying lives and has brought spiritual and physical death. Our pain should propel us to go to the entire world baptizing, teaching, and proclaiming the Good News (see Matthew 28:19-20). We must mourn so much that it causes us to cry out to the One who is life. This is the true character of a follower of Jesus Christ.

It was this profound sense of mourning in Jesus that caused Him to stand over Jerusalem and cry out, "O Jeru-salem, Jerusalem, you who kill the prophets and stone those sent to you, how often I have longed to gather your chil-dren together, as a hen gathers her chicks under her wings, but you were not willing" (23:37). It is that very character trait of mourning that causes His followers to commit their lives to fulfilling His call to help this world know Jesus who died to comfort their mourning.

God calls us into a relationship that is so intimate that our very character is transformed bit by bit into His character. Jesus told us of one of the essential changes that takes place. We mourn. In our mourning, we turn to the one who comforts. In this reality of hope, we are truly "blessed."

QUESTIONS TO CONSIDER

1. What sins around us do we tend to get used to? Why do you think we are so prone to losing our concern over sin?

2. How do you think Jesus would feel about the moral condition of our country? How do you think He would pray?

3. If we were to become sorrowful over the condition of our friends, family, community, and country, how do you think our behavior would change?

4. What hope could Jesus bring to the people in your life who are hurting? What part of Jesus'

message could help them the most? How could you help them see those points of hope?

5. How could you begin expressing an attitude of comfort to those around you who are experiencing the pain of sin?

SPIRIT

Ministry to the Hurting

When Jesus called us to mourn over the sin and pain of this world, He was calling us to more than an emotional response. He was calling us to action. In Matthew 25:31-46 Jesus tells us that our eternal destiny will be determined by what we did with God's call to action. Jesus said that on the Day of Judgment God will separate us like a shepherd separates sheep from goats. Those who help the hurting are the true flock. Those who are all talk and no action are separated for hell. It isn't enough to simply acknowledge someone's pain. True faith gives a cup of cold water, visits the prisoner in jail, clothes the naked, feeds the hungry, and houses the homeless. If the image of God is to be restored in us, we must leave our safety zones and minister to those in need (see vv. 35-46).

This week talk with a spiritual mentor such as a pastor, friend, or Sunday School teacher about opportunities you might have to minister to the hurting. It might be through a Sunday School class. It might be through a soup kitchen. It might be through simple acts of kindness to a neighbor who is hurting. One thing is certain; we cannot claim to follow Christ and refuse to help those who are hurting. That is exactly what Jesus would do. It is exactly what we must do.

SPIRITUAL JOURNEY JOURNAL

WEEK 9

Before you dive into your Spiritual Journey Journal this week, establish a place and a time for you to continue your *personal worship*. Make plans for Sunday as you worship in *community*.

Begin each day this week by reading the scripture passage listed. Try to write a short breath prayer from the passage to use throughout the day. In the evening record your thoughts, insights, and any ways you found God calling you to transformation during the day.

Whether you use the hand or the Lord's Prayer, be sure to invest some of your day in prayer. Feel free to experiment with what works best for you.

My Place for Personal Worship Is . . .

My Time(s) for Personal Worship Is (Are) . . .

My Ministry to the Hurting This Week Might Be . . .

Monday

Scripture: Matthew 5:1-12 (focus on v. 4)
Breath Prayer:

Self-Evaluation—God's call to transformation:

Tuesday

Scripture: Luke 13:31-35

Breath Prayer:

Self-Evaluation—God's call to transformation:

Wednesday

Scripture: John 11:17-43

Breath Prayer:

Self-Evaluation—God's call to transformation:

Thursday

Scripture: Genesis 6:1-6

Breath Prayer:

Self-Evaluation—God's call to transformation:

Friday

Scripture: Psalm 119:135-136

Breath Prayer:

Self-Evaluation—God's call to transformation:

Saturday

Scripture: Psalm 126:4-6

Breath Prayer:

Self-Evaluation—God's call to transformation:

Sunday

Before leaving for church, read today's scripture passage, write out and pray your breath prayer, and ask God to draw near to you. Use the sections below to guide you on this Sabbath Day as you worship and spend time with God.

Scripture: Isaiah 25:7-9

Breath Prayer:

God's tithe (my income this week x 10 percent): $_____

God, I trust You more than money and things. I present Your tithe as an act of worship.

Insights from Sunday School/Bible Study/Small-Group Time:

Preparing for Worship:

During worship, I need You to do this in my heart . . .

As I come to worship, I need You to know . . .

Insights from Worship:

Reflecting on this Sabbath . . .

Today, God, You showed me . . .

This week I want You to do this in my heart . . .

Self-Evaluation—God's call to transformation:

TEN

MEEKNESS

TRUTH

It is impossible for people to restore themselves to God's image. That is a job for the Holy Spirit. Jesus says in Matthew 5:5, "Blessed are the meek, for they will inherit the earth." What a statement! The people who are going to be blessed are the meek.

We often misunderstand what Jesus was saying. Meekness is not simply a quiet response but an appropriate response. When I should be angry, I am angry. When I should be joyful, I am joyful. When I should be silent, I am silent. When I should be forceful, I am forceful. That is a tall order.

To understand just how difficult our situation is, we must understand how sin has impaired our ability to respond appropriately. Paul says in Romans 8:7, "The sinful mind is hostile to God. It does not submit to God's law, nor can it do so." It is set on its own desires. It wants what it wants. Basically, it is selfish. That makes an appropriate response all but impossible. Sure there are times when we want something that happens to be the right thing. However, meekness is not an occasional characteristic. It is a way of approaching the world. Jesus is telling us that consistently responding appropriately (meekness) brings blessings.

Meekness was not highly valued in the Roman Empire of Jesus' day. Meekness is equally underappreciated today. *Winning Through Meekness* probably wouldn't make the *New York Times'* best seller list. Let's face it. Our fallen nature wants its own way. That is why Paul says, "What a wretched man I am! Who will rescue me from this body of death? Thanks be to God—through Jesus Christ our Lord!" (7:24-25).

Meekness is going to take divine intervention. A consistently appropriate response is impossible without the Spirit. "For if you live according to the sinful nature, you will die; but if by the Spirit you put to death the misdeeds of the body, you will live" (8:13). If I am left to fix the problem myself, I will never be blessed because meekness (a consistently appropriate response) is not what I naturally do.

I was about four years old when the extent of my inappropriate responses began to show its ugly head. The big kids were playing Wiffle ball and I was on the sidelines trying to get in on the action. In the middle of this family event some neighborhood bullies arrived. They loved to disrupt the little kids and their game. Their teasing struck that selfish, meek-less area deep inside and I snapped. I grabbed the Wiffle ball bat and tore off after these middle school kids with all the fury of a full-grown man. I swung the bat and gnashed my teeth with the viciousness of a bulldog. Terrified by the sight, they ran for their lives. It had taken two older brothers and a couple cousins to keep me from doing great bodily harm to those boys.

It was only Wiffle ball! But the selfish heart just knows it's been offended. Appropriate or not, it's time to fight!

We have all been there. The situation grows more and more complex and our frustrations grow proportionately. In the middle of the situation, we begin to feel like all of life hangs in the balance of these few moments. And then, something inside of us cracks and we become monsters bent on destruction. In those moments of insanity we experience the depth of our depravity. We are not meek. Our responses are not naturally appropriate. They are self-motivated, self-serving, and out of control.

However, Jesus says, blessed are those who have an appropriate response. And then, He showed us what that looks like. To the woman at the well He showed incredible kindness and compassion (John 4). However, when He entered the Temple, He overturned the money changers' tables because they had violated God's house of prayer (chap. 2). To the woman caught in adultery He showed forgiveness and compassion (chap. 8). But, to the Pharisees Jesus hurled accusations of corrupt hearts (Matthew 23:27-29). In one moment Jesus calls Peter "Satan" (16:23) and in another He showers him with forgiveness when they meet after the Resurrection (John 21).

In these times, Jesus shows us the secret. Where there is repentance there is grace. Where there is arrogance there is confrontation. In all these circumstances, God is seeking our repentance and offering us the hope of restoration to His image. These are the balancing guidelines of meekness. The appropriateness of the response is directly linked to God's desire to restore His image in us. From one act of transformation to another, our character looks more like Him and less like our naturally selfish selves.

"Blessed are the meek, for they will inherit the earth" (Matthew 5:5). We don't have to wait until we get to heaven to have God's image restored. Meekness is a *now* thing that results in influence, or leadership. People will be blessed here and now as inheritors of the earth when they allow the Holy Spirit to give them the ability to respond appropriately.

Begin praying now that God will overcome the battle going on within your heart and mind. Your needs and wants fight for control of your decisions. However, the Spirit needs control. If God gains control over your heart and mind, you will respond with His meekness instead of selfishness. You will respond appropriately and you will be blessed. People will trust you because they will know what to expect from you. People will love you because you will treat them appropriately. In these restored relationships, God can raise you to leadership. His Spirit will have begun the transformation of your image. His love will come out of you instead of your selfishness. In that meekness, you will find true blessing.

QUESTIONS TO CONSIDER

1. How well do you handle your emotions? Do you tend to respond appropriately, or do you tend to overreact or underreact?

2. Has God ever given you special strength to deal with difficult situations? How did your responses surprise you? What did you do different from before? What did God have to do in order to help you respond appropriately?

3. How much time do you invest in spiritual nurturing (i.e., personal worship, ministry, sacrificial obedience, fasting, etc.)? What relationship do you see between the time you spend (or don't spend) and the Spirit's control over your responses?

4. How might you begin to increase your reliance on God to help you respond appropriately?

Take a few minutes and write a prayer asking God to help you deal with the temptation to respond inappropriately. Ask Him to strengthen you with His Spirit. Ask Him to convict you when you overreact or underreact. Thank Him for what He is doing in your life as He transforms your moral image into His likeness.

SPIRIT

Unseen Acts of Kindness

Jesus taught us that when we show kindness to others we show kindness to Him (Matthew 25:40). It is one of the ways we connect with God. Every time we lock eyes with someone who is hurting, it is as if we are locking eyes with Jesus himself. Jesus taught us to show kindness in ways that keep our actions private. We aren't to show off or do acts of kindness for praise or recognition (6:1-4). In fact we are to practice the spiritual discipline of unseen acts of kindness. This week make a point each day to do something for someone without the person knowing who did it. You might clean the house, do the dishes, or something else at home. You might mow the neighbors' yard while they are gone. You might pay the toll for the car behind you. You might even pay for the lunch of someone across the room at your favorite restaurant. Won't he or she be surprised when the waitress doesn't bring a bill!

What's the point? You are drawing near to God by showing the same mercy He has extended to you. With each act of kindness just whisper a simple prayer. "This is for You, Lord."

SPIRITUAL JOURNEY JOURNAL

WEEK 10

Before you dive into your Spiritual Journey Journal this week, establish a place and a time for you to continue your *personal worship*. Make plans for Sunday as you worship in *community*.

Begin each day this week by reading the scripture passage listed. Try to write a short breath prayer from the passage to use throughout the day. In the evening record your thoughts, insights, and any ways you found God calling you to transformation during the day.

Whether you use the hand or the Lord's Prayer, be sure to invest some of your day in prayer. Feel free to experiment with what works best for you.

My Place for Personal Worship Is . . .

My Time(s) for Personal Worship Is (Are) . . .

My Ministry to the Hurting This Week Might Be . . .

Monday

Scripture: Matthew 5:1-12 (focus on v. 5)
Breath Prayer:

Self-Evaluation—God's call to transformation:

Today's Unseen Act of Kindness:

Tuesday

Scripture: Romans 8:6-8
Breath Prayer:

Self-Evaluation—God's call to transformation:

Today's Unseen Act of Kindness:

Wednesday

Scripture: Psalm 4:4-5
Breath Prayer:

Self-Evaluation—God's call to transformation:

Today's Unseen Act of Kindness:

Thursday

Scripture: Roman 7:21-25
Breath Prayer:

Self-Evaluation—God's call to transformation:

Today's Unseen Act of Kindness:

Friday

Scripture: 1 Timothy 2:8
Breath Prayer:

Self-Evaluation—God's call to transformation:

Today's Unseen Act of Kindness:

Saturday

Scripture: Romans 8:11-15
Breath Prayer:

Self-Evaluation—God's call to transformation:

Today's Unseen Act of Kindness:

Sunday

Before leaving for church, read today's scripture passage, write out and pray your breath prayer, and ask God to draw near to you. Use the sections below to guide you on this Sabbath Day as you worship and spend time with God.

Scripture: Psalm 103:2-5

Breath Prayer:

God's tithe (my income this week x 10 percent): $_____

God, I trust You more than money and things. I present Your tithe as an act of worship.

Insights from Sunday School/Bible Study/Small-Group Time:

Preparing for Worship:

During worship, I need You to do this in my heart . . .

As I come to worship, I need You to know . . .

Insights from Worship:

Reflecting on this Sabbath . . .

Today, God, You showed me . . .

This week I want You to do this in my heart . . .

Self-Evaluation—God's call to transformation:

Today's Unseen Act of Kindness:

ELEVEN

HUNGER AND THIRST FOR RIGHTEOUSNESS

TRUTH

The room was full of pastors and we were here for training. Like every other pastor in the room I was quite confident that this would be another one of those seminars on church growth that I would take back to my church and file away with all the other good ideas. However, something very different took place. The speaker, Dr. Dan Boone,* pastor of College Church of the Nazarene in Bourbonnais, Illinois, took the podium and began openly sharing about his struggle to stay spiritually alive. I was on the edge of my seat. I knew all too well what he was talking about.

It doesn't take too many days of serving people with high expectations before you reach the bottom of your spiritual barrel. I had been struggling with Jesus' statements about our righteousness needing to surpass that of the Pharisees if we were going to have any part in the kingdom of God (Matthew 5:20). First Peter 2:9-12 hammers home a similar theme when it calls us "a holy nation"

---

*In 2005 Dr. Boone was elected president of Trevecca Nazarene University.

whose lives should cause pagans to "glorify God." We are to be holy, because God is holy (1 Peter 1:16). I wanted this very much. I just wasn't getting it.

Dr. Boone began, "We were created to be thirsty for God. That's what it means to be a living being, a soul, a *nephesh*. You aren't alive spiritually until you are so hungry for more of God that you can't stand it anymore." He went on, "You will know your soul is beginning to wake up when you become absolutely dependent on God for spiritual nourishment. You weren't created for independence but for utter dependence. To be a soul is to be hungry and thirsty for God."

I couldn't write fast enough. I finally understood why I was so dissatisfied with my spiritual life. I was alive! God was drawing closer and closer. The closer He got, the more dissatisfied I was with my spiritual condition. I wanted more. I wanted more of God's holiness. I wanted my character to look more like His. I wanted God and I wanted Him now. I was *hungry and thirsty!* It wasn't a bad thing. It wasn't a sign of spiritual weakness. It was the sound of a spiritual heartbeat.

That afternoon, I began a spiritual and scriptural reevaluation of what I believed about spiritual maturity. I started digging into the Scriptures. Jesus said, "Unless your righteousness surpasses that of the Pharisees and the teachers of the law, you will certainly not enter the kingdom of heaven" (Matthew 5:20).

Jesus' hearers would have recognized this as a very high call indeed. The Pharisees epitomized Law keepers.

They practiced their hyperlegalistic brand of righteousness openly, sharply criticizing the Sadducees who forged an uneasy political compromise with the Romans. They also considered themselves better than most other Jews because the Pharisees meticulously followed the letter of the Law, even when people ended up being hurt by it. The very center of what they were after had changed. Instead of hungering and thirsting for God, they focused on enforcing the tiniest details of the Law. Meanwhile, many Pharisees felt perfectly free to violate the Law's spirit as long as they kept it letter perfect. They missed the fact that the Law was to point people to God. They made the Law their goal rather than the pointer to the Person. When Jesus said our righteousness must be greater than the Pharisees', I realized that Jesus was not talking about hyperlegalism but hyperthirst.

Our righteousness must flow from a hunger and thirst to know God that wells up from deep within us. In John 4:19-24 Jesus tells the woman at the well that the Father desires true worshipers. Jesus is calling us to a blessed life of thirsty adoration. The worship the Father wants is worship from the gut. This worship is driven by an unsatisfied hunger for closeness to God. God wants people whose spirits are deeply hungry and thirsty for intimacy with Him. Jesus calls us to blessedness through hungry worship, thirsty worship, spiritual worship.

In Jeremiah 29:13 God says, "You will seek me and find me when you seek me with all your heart." This is the picture of the awakened soul. The Hebrew word for soul, *nephesh,* is a word picture of hunger and thirst. It is the picture of an open throat, wide open before God, wanting nourishment like a chick begs of its mother. To be a living being is to be hungry and thirsty. God made us for himself, and only He can satisfy our deepest hunger and thirst. This is what it means to be alive. This is what it means to awaken from the dead. Jeremiah promises we will find God when we wake up. We must heed the calling of Ephesians 5:14, "Wake up, O sleeper, rise from the dead, and Christ will shine on you."

This is what Jesus meant when He said that we are blessed. When we are hungry and thirsty for righteousness, when we have awakened and have taken our position to receive God's nourishing Spirit, we will be filled. This is why Paul encourages us to be continually "filled with the Spirit" (v. 18). We were created to live under the continual filling of His nourishing, life-giving Spirit.

Our spiritual health, worship, and obedience all depend on standing open-mouthed before God. "Feed me! Give me drink! Fill me with Your Spirit! I can't go on without more of You!" When we seek God like this, we are spiritually alive. We are blessed because we will finally get what we need—intimacy with God as He fills us with His presence.

QUESTIONS TO CONSIDER

1. On a scale of 1 to 10, how hungry and thirsty are you for God? Why do you think you are at this point?

2. How does it make you feel to know that being spiritually alive means being dissatisfied with where you are right now? How will you handle this hunger for more intimacy with God?

3. What things keep you from seeking God whole-heartedly? What distracts your attention from God? How do you think God feels about those things?

4. What do you need to do to increase your thirst for God? Take a few minutes and pray over these things. Ask God to help you rearrange your priorities so that He is truly first.

5. How do you think your spiritual life would improve if you really got hungry for God? What would change? What would improve? What would you do differently?

6. How does it make you feel to know that God wants you to depend completely on Him for

spiritual nourishment? How have you handled your dependency on others in the past? What can you do to make sure you respond to God's call for dependence in a healthy way?

SPIRIT

Fasting

This week we are going to focus on one of the most powerful spiritual disciplines Jesus taught. He wasn't the first to fast. However, He was clear that deep spiritual conflicts can be addressed through prayer and fasting. Jesus faced and overcame temptation during His 40 days of prayer and fasting in the desert (Matthew 4; Luke 4). He taught His disciples to fast in Matthew 6. They must have learned their lessons well because Acts 13:2-3 shows that the Spirit spoke to the apostles during a fast. He gave them one of the most strategically important directions the young church received. The apostles responded with prayer and fasting and then commissioned Paul and Barnabas for their ministry to the Gentiles (that's most of us).

So what is fasting? It is refusing food (not water) for a set period of time.

Is it healthy to go without food? Most people who are in good health will benefit from a fast. Remember to drink water to keep your body hydrated. If you have questions, consult your physician first.

Those who are experiencing fasting for the first time might consider fasting a meal or for a day. Once you have some experience, consider fasting for more than one day.

If conditions such as pregnancy or diabetes make a total fast unsafe, consider giving up a food that you really enjoy. Some have fasted soft drinks for an entire year. Some teenagers even went so far as to fast pizza! The point is that we are conditioning ourselves to focus completely on God. We are opening ourselves up to His presence by practicing our complete dependence on Him.

SPIRITUAL JOURNEY JOURNAL

WEEK 11

Before you dive into your Spiritual Journey Journal this week, establish a place and a time for you to continue your *personal worship*. Make plans for Sunday as you worship in *community*.

Begin each day this week by reading the scripture passage listed. Try to write a short breath prayer from the passage to use throughout the day. In the evening record your thoughts, insights, and any ways you found God calling you to transformation during the day.

Whether you use the hand or the Lord's Prayer, be sure to invest some of your day in prayer. Feel free to experiment with what works best for you.

My Place for Personal Worship Is . . .

My Time(s) for Personal Worship Is (Are) . . .

My Ministry to the Hurting This Week Might Be . . .

Monday

Scripture: Matthew 5:1-12 (focus on v. 6)

Breath Prayer:

Self-Evaluation—God's call to transformation:

Today's Unseen Act of Kindness:

Tuesday

Scripture: Matthew 5:17-20

Breath Prayer:

Self-Evaluation—God's call to transformation:

Today's Unseen Act of Kindness:

Wednesday

Scripture: John 4:19-24

Breath Prayer:

Self-Evaluation—God's call to transformation:

Today's Unseen Act of Kindness:

Thursday

Scripture: Jeremiah 29:11-13

Breath Prayer:

Self-Evaluation—God's call to transformation:

Today's Unseen Act of Kindness:

Friday

> Scripture: Genesis 2:4-7
>
> Breath Prayer:

Self-Evaluation—God's call to transformation:

Today's Unseen Act of Kindness:

Saturday

> Scripture: Ephesians 5:14
>
> Breath Prayer:

Self-Evaluation—God's call to transformation:

Today's Unseen Act of Kindness:

Sunday

Before leaving for church, read today's scripture passage, write out and pray your breath prayer, and ask God to draw near to you. Use the sections below to guide you on this Sabbath Day as you worship and spend time with God.

> Scripture: Psalm 24:3-6
>
> Breath Prayer:

God's tithe (my income this week x 10 percent): $_____

God, I trust You more than money and things. I present Your tithe as an act of worship.

Insights from Sunday School/Bible Study/Small-Group Time:

Preparing for Worship:

> During worship, I need You to do this in my heart . . .

> As I come to worship, I need You to know . . .

Insights from Worship:

Reflecting on this Sabbath . . .

> Today, God, You showed me . . .

This week I want You to do this in my heart . . .

Self-Evaluation—God's call to transformation:

Today's Unseen Act of Kindness:

RESTORING HIS IMAGE, PART II

TWELVE

LIVING MERCY

TRUTH

I was 13 years old when my image of my perfect family came crashing down. One of my friends had rushed up to me at our church campgrounds. "Kevin, did you know that your brother is chewing tobacco?" I grew up in a family that stressed personal piety, and if my brother was dabbling in something like tobacco, it had much deeper implications—he had turned against his family's values.

I couldn't and I wouldn't believe it. My brother was my protector, my hero. I was instantly filled with anger. I wasn't angry with my brother. I was angry with this horrible liar who would try to say such a thing about my family. I ran to find my brother. I would prove this horrible accusation was hogwash. I knew where my brother was, and I was already yelling his name. There he was. His lip was full of chew and my jaw hung open. My anger stayed and slowly began to shift toward him. Even though the anger was hidden beneath the hurt and disappointment, it was still there.

Over the course of the next few years, my brother sunk deeper and deeper into addictions. With each new pain that he inflicted on himself, he caused an equal amount on his family. My anger grew and slowly transformed into indignation and righteous judgment.

"If he loved us, he wouldn't do these things," I thought. It didn't take much time before I had come to the opinion that somewhere down deep inside I was better than my brother and had a right to be angry with him.

Twenty years later, I sat in a spiritual formation seminar at seminary. The professors forced me to question my confidence with an exercise designed to help us identify places where we had not shown mercy. The anger for my brother still boiled inside. The Lord asked, "If you are so merciful, then why can't you forgive your brother?" This struck me to the core.

I was no better than my brother, just different. The pain he had inflicted on me was the same that I had inflicted on others. Sin is the great equalizer. "For all have sinned and fall short of the glory of God" (Romans 3:23). Jesus calls us to be merciful. At that moment, mercy meant releasing the anger I felt for all that my brother did to himself and those who cared about him. I needed to see my brother as someone to love instead of someone to condemn. My brother needed God's forgiveness. And I needed to forgive him too.

My choice would determine how God would respond to me. I had a decision to make. I would either forgive because I was forgiven. Or I would ignore the great mercy God had shown me and cling to my anger.

Jesus said, "Blessed are the merciful, for they will be shown mercy" (Matthew 5:7). He also told us we will be judged with the same standards we use to judge others (7:1-2).

It makes sense. If I look at God's mercy on my life and choose to treat others with judgment, I will not receive the mercy God offers me. If I live a life of mercy, God will show me mercy. It all depends on how I choose to live. I will either live out the blessing of God and show others mercy, or I will ignore the blessing of God, judge others, and receive judgment.

Sometimes *obligation* masquerades as *mercy*. We may act like we are offering forgiveness when we are actually making someone our servant. He or she owes us for what he or she has done. Instead of showing genuine mercy, we obligate the person because we have said words that sound forgiving. Our actions let him or her know that he or she is still obligated for what was done. At any time we can remind the person of the pain he or she caused. Emotionally the person drops to his or her knees and begs for forgiveness time and time again. It is awesome power to wield. He or she isn't forgiven, only obligated to us.

Jesus, however, taught mercy, not obligation. Mercy doesn't make demands from the other person. Mercy flows from gratitude for the mercy that we have received. I was guilty before God for the sin I committed. And yet, I am forgiven. Who am I to hold you accountable to me for what you have done? I was imprisoned by sin, too, but God forgave me and released me. My freedom was an act of God's mercy. I refuse to take the freedom that God gave me and use it to judge you.

Instead of judgment, I have good news. I know that God loves mercy. To live out this mercy God has shown me, I am an avenue of God's mercy to you. Then, maybe, through the mercy I show you, God will be able to reach you with His love and forgiveness. This is how my mercy becomes a source of blessing. I am shown mercy in the same way I show it. When I show you mercy, God is able to get mercy to you as well!

Jesus wants to restore God's image in us. If we reflect the image of our Creator, we must also reflect His mercy by living the mercy that defined His relationship to us.

QUESTIONS TO CONSIDER

1. Have you ever had a difficult time forgiving someone? What were the circumstances? Why do you think it was so difficult to forgive?

2. Have you ever done something that you feared God would not easily forgive? What about it made you think that it was too horrible for God's mercy?

3. Can you remember when you sought and received God's mercy and forgiveness? What seri-

ous sins had you confessed? What were some of the less serious sins? Did the severity of the sins affect your ability to experience the peace that comes with forgiveness? Why? Why not?

4. How does it make you feel to have someone forgive you for what you did to him or her? Are these emotions similar to how you felt when God for Christ's sake forgave you?

5. Since we know that God judges us based on how we show mercy to others, describe what God's standard of judgment for you looks like.

6. If forgiving someone is choosing to release the person from accountability to you for what he or she has done, have you ever truly forgiven someone? How did humility play a role in your ability to forgive? How did the mercy God showed you play a role?

7. Have you ever shown mercy to someone that others seem unwilling to forgive? How did your mercy and love affect him or her? How did your actions reflect the mercy God loves to show people?

SPIRIT

Focusing Our Spiritual Eyes—Seeing God's Mercy

I took the plunge and had Lasik surgery to correct my extreme nearsightedness. When I lay down on the operating table I couldn't see anything farther away than nine inches. In a matter of moments, the doctor corrected my vision. When I sat up I could tell life was going to be different. I could already see so much more than I could before. I could read the clock on the wall. I could see the doctor's face!

Because the surgery was so fresh, my vision was cloudy for a day or so. However, with each passing hour I could see a little better. The surgery changed the structure of my eyes and my muscles had to learn how to focus with these new eyes. It was tiring at first. I would have to force my eyes to focus. However, over the next few weeks, my eyes became accustomed to the change and focusing became as natural as breathing.

This is a good picture of our attempt to sense God's presence with our spiritual eyes. When we are in

Christ, we know something is very different. We can sense the Spirit of God in ways we never could before. Even though our spiritual vision is a bit cloudy, we finally start getting a glimpse of the true character of God. He is a holy God who balances justice with mercy. There is no need to fear a God like that.

With time, focusing our spiritual eyes on God becomes more familiar. We sense God's leading and prodding. We know when He is calling us to account, and we know when He is pleased with us.

However, life has the tendency to become clouded with difficult circumstances. Sometimes we have to stop and force ourselves to focus on His presence again. It is difficult to step into God's presence when you've been running at full tilt all day. It is difficult to focus your spiritual eyes on His presence when pictures of all that must be done flood your mind. Sometimes, we have to stop and force our spiritual eyes to focus on Him and Him alone.

As you learn to stop and focus your spiritual eyes on Christ, your personal and corporate worship times will become richer and richer. Begin your personal and corporate worship times by forcing yourself to focus on Christ. Clear your mind. Imagine Christ is in the room with you. In the same way your eyes need time to adjust to the light, your spiritual eyes need time to adjust to being in His presence. Look into His eyes. Don't stop until you can clearly picture Him. You will find His eyes are still full of mercy for those who seek Him.

SPIRITUAL JOURNEY JOURNAL

WEEK 12

Before you dive into your Spiritual Journey Journal this week, establish a place and a time for you to continue your *personal worship*. Make plans for Sunday as you worship in *community*.

Begin each day this week by reading the scripture passage listed. Try to write a short breath prayer from the passage to use throughout the day. In the evening record your thoughts, insights, and any ways you found God calling you to transformation during the day.

Make sure to begin each worship time by focusing your spiritual eyes on God. See His mercy and ask Him to transform you in the moments to come.

My Place for Personal Worship Is . . .

My Time(s) for Personal Worship Is (Are) . . .

My Ministry to the Hurting This Week Might Be . . .

Monday

Scripture: Matthew 5:3-11 (focus on v. 7)
Breath Prayer:

Self-Evaluation—God's call to transformation:

Today's Unseen Act of Kindness:

Tuesday

Scripture: Matthew 7:1-2
Breath Prayer:

Self-Evaluation—God's call to transformation:

Today's Unseen Act of Kindness:

Wednesday
     Scripture: Matthew 6:12-15
     Breath Prayer:

Self-Evaluation—God's call to transformation:

Today's Unseen Act of Kindness:

Thursday
     Scripture: Colossians 3:12-13
     Breath Prayer:

Self-Evaluation—God's call to transformation:

Today's Unseen Act of Kindness:

Friday
     Scripture: Micah 6:8
     Breath Prayer:

Self-Evaluation—God's call to transformation:

Today's Unseen Act of Kindness:

Saturday
     Scripture: Matthew 9:10-12
     Breath Prayer:

Self-Evaluation—God's call to transformation:

Today's Unseen Act of Kindness:

Sunday

Before leaving for church, read today's scripture passage, write out and pray your breath prayer, and ask God to draw near to you. Use the sections below to guide you on this Sabbath Day as you worship and spend time with God.

Scripture: Psalm 89:1-4

Breath Prayer:

God's tithe (my income this week x 10 percent): $_____

God, I trust You more than money and things. I present Your tithe as an act of worship.

Insights from Sunday School/Bible Study/Small-Group Time:

Preparing for Worship:

During worship, I need You to do this in my heart . . .

As I come to worship, I need You to know . . .

Insights from Worship:

Reflecting on this Sabbath . . .

Today, God, You showed me . . .

This week I want You to do this in my heart . . .

Self-Evaluation—God's call to transformation:

Today's Unseen Act of Kindness:

THIRTEEN

PURE HEARTS

TRUTH

My family has always enjoyed theme parks. Most of my vacation memories as a child were of Six Flags in St. Louis or Chicago. My father and my older brothers were like supermen. They could handle the highest, fastest, most nauseating roller coasters on the planet. But I wasn't tall enough yet.

We waited in line forever just to get the thrill of a two-minute ride. The lines stretched from the entrance several hundred feet down the walkway. Moreover, there was always the chance that after waiting such a long time, you wouldn't get to ride. There would always be a sandwich board type sign with a Bugs Bunny or Daffy Duck holding his hand up to a certain height. I was sure it was placed there to humiliate the smaller framed. You couldn't get on the ride unless you were taller than the hand of whatever character blocked your way to the entrance. Not only did you have to wait a very long time, but you also had to measure up. This all added up to an intimidating, frustrating experience.

When we hear Jesus say, "Blessed are the pure in heart, for they will see God" (Matthew 5:8), we may get that same feeling of not measuring up. We want to be a part of the Kingdom. We want His image restored in us, but how can we measure up to this one? We know ourselves too well. Bad attitudes, short tempers, self-centeredness, faithlessness, doubting; these things sound much more familiar. Heart purity? No way!

So, why would Jesus put such a call in front of us? Is He trying to humiliate us by making us stand underneath His measuring stick to show us just how far we fall short? Is He calling us to enter a lifelong search for something we will only have in eternity? Is He maybe, just maybe, calling us to allow Him to do something in us that we cannot do for ourselves? I believe this last option is the truth.

James 4:7-10 says:

> Submit yourselves, then, to God. Resist the devil, and he will flee from you. Come near to God and he will come near to you. Wash your hands, you sinners, and purify your hearts, you double-minded. Grieve, mourn and wail. Change your laughter to mourning and your joy to gloom. Humble yourselves before the Lord, and he will lift you up.

Transforming our hearts from sinful to pure begins with two actions: (1) We resist the devil and (2) we draw near to God. This is how we allow Him to take over the transformation process. And He does!

When He draws near to us, He enables us to do two more things we were unable to do without Him. First, we can wash our hands (v. 8). He gives the faith we need to accept the grace of forgiveness. In this moment the purity of our hearts begins. This is why Paul says:

> I pray that out of his glorious riches he may strengthen you with power through his Spirit in your inner being, so that Christ may dwell in your hearts through faith *(Ephesians 3:16-17a)*.

As we receive Christ, we are being purified in the sense of having our sins forgiven. Love takes hold in us. That is why Paul defines this part of our purification as "being rooted and established in love" (v. 17*b*). Forgiveness is the beginning of our "purity in heart." We are rooted and established in love.

There is a second thing God enables us to do when we come to Christ. He invites, "Purify your hearts, you double-minded" (James 4:8). Becoming pure in heart is a matter of resolving our divided love for God. We love God, but other loves compete with Him.

We love God, but we may love ourselves just as much, if not more. We love God, but we love our family and may value their opinion more than His commands. We love God, but we may love our social standing or popularity more. We love God, *but* . . . you get the picture.

The Spirit must do something in the deepest caverns of our soul. He must purify our hearts so that our love is pure, full, and undividedly for God first of all. This is why Paul finishes his prayer with these words:

> And I pray that you, being rooted and established in love, may have power, together with all the saints, to grasp how wide and long and high and deep is the love of Christ, and to know this love that surpasses knowledge—that you may be filled to the measure of all the fullness of God.

Now to him who is able to do immeasurably more than all we ask or imagine, according to his power that is at work within us, to him be glory in the church and in Christ Jesus throughout all generations, for ever and ever! Amen *(Ephesians 3:17-21)*.

Paul prays that we would experience the heights of love for God available to us that go far beyond knowledge. This highest love for God is defined as "filled to the measure of all the fullness of God" (v. 19). God can completely fill us with a love for Him that unites division of our affections into a single focus on Him. We can be completely set apart for God, completely in love with Him, undivided in our minds and united in our affection.

Why was this so important? Because this purity of heart repairs the damage sin (loving ourselves and what we want more than God) has wreaked on our relationships. First Timothy 1:3-5 teaches that a pure heart is the source of love. The command here is to resist the pointless bickering over differences of opinion. The way to do that is to love from a pure heart. Purity of heart allows us to love people, even when we disagree with them.

First Peter 1:22—2:3 shows how purity of heart leads to good relationships and a greater thirst for God. A pure heart awakens us, makes us thirsty for God, and enables us to love others. No wonder Jesus said, "Blessed are the pure in heart" (Matthew 5:8). God can deliver us from double-minded, halfhearted "love" for God to single-minded, Spirit-given, pure-hearted devotion to God. Why? Those with pure hearts are blessed because they will see God.

What is Jesus talking about, "seeing God"? Will we begin seeing hallucinations, mirages, apparitions, or visions?

Revelation 22:1, 3-5 can help us understand what Jesus means.

> Then the angel showed me the river of the water of life, as clear as crystal, flowing from the throne of God and of the Lamb. . . . No longer will there be any curse. The throne of God and of the Lamb will be in the city, and his servants will serve him. They will see his face, and his name will be on their foreheads. There will be no more night. They will not need the light of a lamp or the light of the sun, for the Lord God will give them light. And they will reign for ever and ever.

This is a picture of our reward: eternal life. The blessed "will see his face" (v. 4). How did they get there? Jesus tells us, "Blessed are the pure in heart, for they will see God" (Matthew 5:8).

Purity of heart is a *must* for those who would receive the rewards. However, purity of heart is *given* by God. The rewards we receive are available because of God's grace in restoring His image in us. Those rewards center on walking with God, just like He intended in Eden.

QUESTIONS TO CONSIDER

1. What are the areas of life that people tend to value more than their love for God? Why do you think these things compete with God for our love?

2. Think back to times when your relationships have struggled. What role did selfishness play in these times? How did selfishness affect you? How did selfishness affect the other people in your relationship? How could a pure heart or a pure love for God have made a difference?

3. Describe how you felt about God when you met Christ? How did you feel when you were "rooted and established in love"?

4. When did you begin realizing your love for God needed to deepen? How did that make you feel? What have you done about this? Write a prayer that describes what you want Him to do.

5. A pure heart is essential to see God. The good news is that this purity is a gift from God. On a scale of 1 to 10, how pure is your love for God now?

SPIRIT

Plan for Growth

Purity of heart is the result of God's work in our lives. God does not impose this on us, however. He seeks our permission and cooperation so our love for Him is real. He invites us to receive all that He has for us. That means intentionally placing ourselves in the flow of His Spirit and being open to His leading. One of the greatest ways you can intentionally position yourself to receive the transforming flow of the Spirit is to create and follow a plan for growth.

A plan for growth is a daily action plan. It begins by honestly assessing your strengths and weaknesses. Once you have identified these, ask what actions you can take that would allow God to help you strengthen your weaknesses. It is important that these actions be things that you can do. To say, "I want my spouse to be more patient with my overeating" is not within your control. To say, "I want to talk with my spouse about the stress I am facing" *is* within your control.

Once you have identified the areas of weakness and the actions you can take to help these areas, *schedule* them on your plan for growth. Some actions will be daily activities, some weekly, and some others monthly. Whatever the timeframe, put them on your schedule and stick to it.

Your plan for growth should cover spiritual, physical, mental, relational, and financial areas of life. You can make it as simple or detailed as you like. Some people set aside a week every year to review and write their plan for the upcoming year. The week between Christmas and New Year's Day works for many. Choose a time that works best for you. Begin your first plan for growth this week.

A Personal Plan for Growth work sheet and an example of a completed plan are included in the appendix.

SPIRITUAL JOURNEY JOURNAL

WEEK 13

Before you dive into your Spiritual Journey Journal this week, establish a place and a time for you to continue your *personal worship*. Make plans for Sunday as you worship in *community*.

Begin each day this week by reading the scripture passage listed. Try to write a short breath prayer from the passage to use throughout the day. In the evening record your thoughts, insights, and any ways you found God calling you to transformation during the day.

Begin working on your personal plan for growth. Be honest with yourself about those areas where God is trying to stretch you.

My Place for Personal Worship Is . . .

My Time(s) for Personal Worship Is (Are) . . .

My Ministry to the Hurting This Week Might Be . . .

Monday

Scripture: Matthew 5:3-11 (focus on v. 8)
Breath Prayer:

Self-Evaluation—God's call to transformation:

Today's Unseen Act of Kindness:

Tuesday

    Scripture: James 4:4-10

    Breath Prayer:

Self-Evaluation—God's call to transformation:

Today's Unseen Act of Kindness:

Wednesday

    Scripture: 1 Timothy 1:3-5

    Breath Prayer:

Self-Evaluation—God's call to transformation:

Today's Unseen Act of Kindness:

Thursday

    Scripture: 1 Peter 1:22—2:3

    Breath Prayer:

Self-Evaluation—God's call to transformation:

Today's Unseen Act of Kindness:

Friday

    Scripture: Revelation 22:1-5

    Breath Prayer:

Self-Evaluation—God's call to transformation:

Today's Unseen Act of Kindness:

Saturday

    Scripture: Psalm 51:10

    Breath Prayer:

Self-Evaluation—God's call to transformation:

Today's Unseen Act of Kindness:

Sunday

Before leaving for church, read today's scripture passage, write out and pray your breath prayer, and ask God to draw near to you. Use the sections below to guide you on this Sabbath Day as you worship and spend time with God.

Scripture: Psalm 73:1

Breath Prayer:

God's tithe (my income this week x 10 percent): $_____

God, I trust You more than money and things. I present Your tithe as an act of worship.

Insights from Sunday School/Bible Study/Small-Group Time:

Preparing for Worship:

During worship, I need You to do this in my heart . . .

As I come to worship, I need You to know . . .

Insights from Worship:

Reflecting on this Sabbath . . .

Today, God, You showed me . . .

This week I want You to do this in my heart . . .

Self-Evaluation—God's call to transformation:

Today's Unseen Act of Kindness:

FOURTEEN

PEACEMAKERS

TRUTH

If there is one inescapable picture in Genesis, it is that God created us for relationships. Sin's most devastating effect is that it turned us from partners into adversaries. God intended for us to live peacefully, yet we are plagued by conflict, blame, and shame.

Jesus calls us to stop the conflict as part of the Sermon on the Mount. He says, "Blessed are the peacemakers, for they will be called sons of God" (Matthew 5:9). We look like our Heavenly Father as He works through us to bring peace.

Peacemaking is characteristic of the family of God. The writer of Hebrews said:

> Make every effort to live in peace with all men and to be holy; without holiness no one will see the Lord. See to it that no one misses the grace of God and that no bitter root grows up to cause trouble and defile many *(12:14)*.

Living at peace flows from God's character: *holiness*—the perfect balance of love and justice. As sons and daughters of God, how can we tolerate factions, divisions, and backbiting in our lives? The bitterness from these things causes people to miss God's grace. Peacemaking is one way God brings His grace to those around us. Whether we are dealing with friends or enemies, we are called to be peacemakers (Proverbs 16:7).

Paul explains how peace can help us be sure that our love is sincere.

> Do not repay anyone evil for evil. Be careful to do what is right in the eyes of everybody. *If it is possible, as far as it depends on you, live at peace with everyone.* Do not take revenge, my friends, but leave room for God's wrath, for it is written: "It is mine to avenge; I will repay," says the Lord. On the contrary: "If your enemy is hungry, feed him; if he is thirsty, give him something to drink. In doing this, you will heap burning coals on his head." Do not be overcome by evil, but overcome evil with good *(Romans 12:17-21, emphasis added)*.

Paul's ending words are reminiscent of Jesus' reminder that when we feed the hungry or give a drink to the thirsty, we do these things to Jesus (Matthew 25:35). Our peacemaking is always about how we treat Jesus. We never face an enemy without facing Christ. We choose to love each other because we love Christ. We cannot separate love for God from peace with each other. We cannot claim to love God and refuse to reconcile with each other.

Peacemaking is easy to talk about but difficult to do. Jesus knew we couldn't do it alone. The gift of the Spirit is the source of peace (John 14:26-27). Many times it takes the Spirit's intervention to give us the strength to be peacemakers.

I was a youth pastor when this reality hit home. In my denomination all staff must resign when the senior pastor resigns. I went to an Easter service with a pastor I loved. By the end of the day, the church fired this man of God. I was stunned and hurt. I loved the members of the congregation, and I loved the pastor.

I felt like a child in a nasty divorce. My senior pastor was deeply hurt and had little strength to help with my pain. The congregation was hurting too. They could not be my source of strength either.

Suddenly I found myself thrust into the role of peacemaker. The board asked me to stay until the new pastor came. I was too young and naive to know that I didn't have the skills for this. For the next six months I awoke with the same prayer, "God, I am at the bottom of my barrel and I have nothing to give. Give me the strength to give these people what they need."

Person after person came through my office. I had to listen, comfort, and counsel. I did all I could to encourage them to stick in there and trust God.

After awhile peace would come over them. They would thank me and leave. I would lie across my desk and pray, "O God, help me. I can't do this anymore."

Then the next person would call.

On one particular morning, I was preparing to meet a board member for lunch. I was so discouraged that I wanted to crawl in a hole and hide. I prayed the prayer again. "O God, help me. I am at the bottom of my barrel. I know this person needs to find Your peace. Please help me make it through this lunch."

As I sat and waited for the person to arrive, something happened. It wasn't a spiritually high moment. It was simply the provision I needed for that person. The member came, we talked, I counseled, and the member left. God provided strength through His Spirit so that I could be a source of peace even in the middle of my pain.

Sometimes this is how we deliver peace to others. At other times we deliver peace by refusing to let our own conflicts stay unresolved. Jesus was so serious about this kind of peacemaking that He followed the blessing on peacemakers with the command to resolve our conflicts before we come to worship (Matthew 5:23). He even gave us a plan to make peace.

> If your brother sins against you, go and show him his fault, just between the two of you. If he listens to you, you have won your brother over. But if he will not listen, take one or two others along, so that "every matter may be established by the testimony of two or three witnesses." If he refuses to listen to them, tell it to the church; and if he refuses to listen even to the church, treat him as you would a pagan or a tax collector *(18:15-17)*.

First, we need to go directly to the person with whom we have a conflict. We are to go quietly. Most conflicts are more easily resolved when we refuse to talk it over with others first. We need to practice saying, "I am sorry that I hurt you. You are important to me. You are my spiritual brother (or sister). You will always be more important to me than any disagreement we might have."

If that doesn't work, it is possible that we aren't being heard or we aren't listening. So, Jesus instructs us to bring witnesses to help us stay away from blame and shame. Our goal is to reconcile. We aren't seeking an apology. We are offering reconciliation because God's forgiveness and grace are directly related to our forgiveness of others.

If these two steps don't work, then it is time to bring in the church. Take your pastor or mutually respected spiritual leader. If that doesn't work, Jesus counsels us to treat the person as an outsider.

It is important to note that Jesus didn't condemn tax collectors. Matthew, whose Gospel contains this teaching, had been a tax collector. Jesus focused on helping them find forgiveness and healing. That's right. Even when they reject our peacemaking, we are never to give up. In fact, we are to intensify our efforts.

The Spirit brings peace. Peacemaking is part of God's image being restored in us. We are blessed because peace undoes the effects of the sin that poison relationships. It takes God's Spirit to change us from fighters to peacemakers. We are His children. We are peacemakers.

QUESTIONS TO CONSIDER

1. Have you ever experienced a broken relationship? What kinds of things caused the break? What was so difficult about holding the relationship together?

2. How do you handle it when people attack you? What emotions do you feel? How do you relate to the person who turned on you?

3. How would becoming a peacemaker change the way you deal with broken relationships and attacks that come your way?

4. Have you applied Jesus' plan for peacemaking to these situations? What are the fears you have about doing this? How do you think following Jesus' plan for peacemaking would affect the other people involved?

5. How does it make you feel to know that you cannot tolerate divided relationships and still claim to love God? How will this impact what you do about the broken relationships in your life? How will this impact how you handle conflict in the future?

6. Write in the names of people you would feel uneasy meeting on the street because of unresolved conflict. Use this as your prayer list for the next few weeks. Ask God to give you the opportunity to heal these relationships in the days to come. That might mean asking God to give you the ability to forgive or the courage to take the first step in resolving the conflict.

SPIRIT

Conflict Resolution

One essential spiritual discipline in believers' lives is conflict resolution. What does conflict resolution have to do with positioning myself to receive the flow of God's Spirit? Unresolved conflict chokes the flow of God's Spirit into my life. Jesus told us that unresolved conflict hinders our worship so much that we must take care of it before we try to worship (Matthew 5:23). Some believers settle for a fake peace rather than authentic healing and restoration.

Jesus provided a clear conflict resolution model in Matthew 18:

1. Go directly to the person, quietly and alone. "If your brother sins against you, go and show him his fault, just between the two of you" (v. 15).

2. If the person doesn't accept your attempt to reconcile, take one or two others with you to make sure your communication doesn't break

down. "But if he will not listen, take one or two others along, so that 'every matter may be established by the testimony of two or three witnesses'" (v. 16).

3. If the second attempt at reconciliation doesn't work, take a pastor or other spiritual mentor that both of you respect. "If he refuses to listen to them, tell it to the church" (v. 17).

4. If after all these attempts the other party refuses to resolve the conflict, call the church to pray. "And if he refuses to listen even to the church, treat him as you would a pagan or a tax collector" (v. 17).

Remember that Jesus was a friend to tax collectors (Matthew 11:19). But only one, Matthew, who left that profession to follow Christ, was in His inner circle.

Now that you know the steps, what should you communicate when trying to resolve the conflict? In the verses preceding these instructions, Jesus gave us the context for most conflicts. They often arise when we value something more than the person with whom we are fighting.

Peacemaking begins with the little things. Jesus warned us not to call someone "raca" (5:22). In our day, this would be the equivalent of calling someone an idiot. While that sounds petty, remember that when Jesus wanted to change someone's future He changed the person's name: Levi to Matthew, Simon to Peter, and Saul to Paul. What we call someone communicates what we believe about him or her.

The teaching about reconciliation comes in the middle of this command to value all people as God values them. They are valuable to Him, and we must work to keep our relationship with them whole.

With this in mind, many have found it helpful to say something like this when going to resolve a conflict. "I realize that we have some unresolved conflicts. I just want you to know that I value you more than any disagreement we might have. I want us to find a way to heal our relationship. That is important to me. I don't expect you to agree with me and I'm sure I may not always agree with you. However, that shouldn't keep us from loving each other. Would you be open to spending some time talking about this?"

It may take some time to finally work through all the hurt feelings and disagreements. However, when you begin the conversation affirming their value and your commitment to love them, it makes the work of conflict resolution far less painful.

SPIRITUAL JOURNEY JOURNAL

WEEK 14

Before you dive into your Spiritual Journey Journal this week, establish a place and a time for you to continue your *personal worship*. Make plans for Sunday as you worship in *community*.

Begin each day this week by reading the scripture passage listed. Try to write a short breath prayer from the passage to use throughout the day. In the evening record your thoughts, insights, and any ways you found God calling you to transformation during the day.

Continue working on your personal plan for growth. Be honest with yourself about those areas where God is trying to stretch you. Make a special effort to identify any relationships in your life that have unresolved conflict. Ask God to give you the grace and courage to begin resolving those conflicts.

My Place for Personal Worship Is . . .

My Time(s) for Personal Worship Is (Are) . . .

My Ministry to the Hurting This Week Might Be . . .

Monday

Scripture: Matthew 5:3-11 (focus on v. 9)
Breath Prayer:

Self-Evaluation—God's call to transformation:

Today's Unseen Act of Kindness:

Tuesday

Scripture: Matthew 18:15-17
Breath Prayer:

Self-Evaluation—God's call to transformation:

Today's Unseen Act of Kindness:

Wednesday

Scripture: John 14:25-27

Breath Prayer:

Self-Evaluation—God's call to transformation:

Today's Unseen Act of Kindness:

Thursday

Scripture: Proverbs 16:7
Breath Prayer:

Self-Evaluation—God's call to transformation:

Today's Unseen Act of Kindness:

Friday

Scripture: Romans 12:17-21
Breath Prayer:

Self-Evaluation—God's call to transformation:

Today's Unseen Act of Kindness:

Saturday

Scripture: Hebrews 12:14-15
Breath Prayer:

Self-Evaluation—God's call to transformation:

Today's Unseen Act of Kindness:

Sunday

Before leaving for church, read today's scripture passage, write out and pray your breath prayer, and ask God to draw near to you. Use the sections below to guide you on this Sabbath Day as you worship and spend time with God.

Scripture: Mark 9:50

Breath Prayer:

God's tithe (my income this week x 10 percent): $_____

God, I trust You more than money and things. I present Your tithe as an act of worship.

Insights from Sunday School/Bible Study/Small-Group Time:

Preparing for Worship:

During worship, I need You to do this in my heart . . .

As I come to worship, I need You to know . . .

Insights from Worship:

Reflecting on this Sabbath . . .

Today, God, You showed me . . .

This week I want You to do this in my heart . . .

Self-Evaluation—God's call to transformation:

Today's Unseen Act of Kindness:

FIFTEEN

LIVING IN THE LINE OF THE PROPHETS

TRUTH

I take seriously my responsibility to help my sons learn the right way to live. Sometimes I take it a little too seriously. Andrew is the oldest. I've been teaching him leadership principles since he was in kindergarten.

"What's the number one rule of being a leader, Andrew?" As I dropped him off to school we'd go through this ritual.

"People do what people see."

I'd praise him. He grinned with the pride of a Nobel prize winner. Then I'd say, "What does that mean, Andrew?"

He'd grin and say, "I don't have a clue!"

Then we'd laugh.

Eventually he learned this law of leadership meant to set a good example. By the end of first grade he had learned to tease me.

"It means that if someone else misbehaves, I should do what they do," and then he'd laugh.

I was thrilled. If he understood the principle well enough to twist it into a joke, he really understood it. I began adding other principles.

One day, after getting into trouble with his teacher, Andrew and I had a serious conversation. "Don't you remember all the principles I've taught you?"

His face contorted and his voice broke with honest frustration. His words came slowly as he struggled to put what he was feeling into a sentence. "Dad, . . . I . . . uh . . . I get stuff—stuff like 'people do what people see'—I get that in my head and it gets all mixed up, . . . and I . . . uh . . . I just can't keep it all straight. I just don't know what to do!"

He was so exasperated. I had to step back and look at who I was talking to. This was a young boy, not a 24-year-old who could incorporate a thousand principles into his behavior. It was enough for my son to remember his lunchbox before leaving for school.

Sometimes this is how we feel when we are learning to incorporate Jesus' teachings into our lives. "It gets all mixed up," and we "don't know what to do!" Jesus must have understood this because He gave a clear idea of what it means to be a follower. He says we are blessed when we apply all these teachings in such a way that people treat us the same way they treated Him. This sounds fine until we remember the crowds persecuted Jesus just like they did the earlier prophets. Listen to Jesus' words:

> Blessed are those who are persecuted because of righteousness, for theirs is the kingdom of heaven. Blessed are you when people insult you, persecute you and falsely say all kinds of evil against you because of me. Rejoice and be glad, because great is your reward in heaven, for in the

same way they persecuted the prophets who were before you *(Matthew 5:10-12)*.

The danger is that we would learn just enough to change what we know, but not enough to change what we do. Contemporary culture expects people to compartmentalize their spiritual journeys. Most people don't care what you believe as long as you keep it to yourself. When that happens, we have missed the entire point of the Sermon on the Mount. True blessing comes when you really *are* meek, when you really *are* hungry and thirsty for righteousness, when you really *are* sorrowful over sin. Jesus concludes the Beatitudes with this call to incorporate *all* the teachings in our lives so others see Him. We join the ranks of prophets, not as fortune-tellers, but as people who speak God's Word *and* live God's Word, even when it is unpopular. Jesus said, "Blessed are you when people . . . persecute you . . . because of me" (v. 11).

First Peter 4 tells us that when we live this kind of righteousness we participate in the sufferings of Jesus.

Dear friends, do not be surprised at the painful trial you are suffering, as though something strange were happening to you. But rejoice that you participate in the sufferings of Christ, so that you may be overjoyed when his glory is revealed. If you are insulted because of the name of Christ, you are blessed, for the Spirit of glory and of God rests on you. If you suffer, it should not be as a murderer or thief or any other kind of criminal, or even as a meddler. However, if you suffer as a Christian, do not be ashamed, but praise God that you bear that name *(vv. 12-16).*

This is probably the most difficult part of following Jesus. Most of us want a Savior who promises utopia. However, if you are going to follow Jesus, you are going to be treated like Jesus was treated. How long will this last? Jesus told us, "When you are persecuted in one place, flee to another. I tell you the truth, you will not finish going through the cities of Israel before the Son of Man comes" (Matthew 10:23). It won't end until Jesus returns to finalize the establishment of His eternal kingdom. The life of a believer is to live out the teachings of Jesus despite persecution and rejection. It is the blessed life of being a prophet.

Jesus lived this kind of life all the way to the Cross. A thief, the Pharisees, and the crowd who watched Him die hurled insults at Him. He knows what it means to be persecuted. When He says, "Anyone who does not take his cross and follow me is not worthy of me" (v. 38), He calls us to live righteously in the face of opposition the way He did. When we do, we are blessed.

When you began your relationship with God, the Holy Spirit began transforming your character to be like Christ. Jesus came to give you life in its fullest degree (John 10:10). He placed His Holy Spirit in you to empower you to be His witnesses (Acts 1:8). The Holy Spirit restores God's image in you. It isn't restored merely because we believe certain things. God's image is restored because of what He changes in you. What is inside comes out in your behavior (Matthew 12:34; Luke 6:45). We know that we are being restored, when like the prophets, we express righteousness no matter what the personal cost.

QUESTIONS TO CONSIDER

1. Look back through the chapters on Restoring His Image. Which of these areas seems the most difficult for you? Why?

2. How closely does your behavior reflect the teachings of Jesus you've learned in this course? What area is God leading you to improve now?

3. Have you ever faced rejection or persecution for a spiritual stand you took? What were the circumstances? How did you handle the pressure? What advice would you give to others who face similar circumstances?

4. Knowing that persecution won't end until Jesus returns, what advice would you give new Christians who expect life to be perfect now that they've been saved? What parts of that advice do you need to hear?

5. How does it make you feel to know that you are actually participating in the sufferings of Jesus? Why?

6. Since God's forgiveness begins a journey to transform us into His image, what are the next steps in your transformation?

SPIRIT

Accountability Prayer Partners

Three things keep us on track in our relationship with Christ: confession, intimacy with God, and accountability. This is what I call living in the spiritual C.I.A. Confession is the willingness to admit when and how I am tempted or if I sin.

Intimacy is seeking friendship with God. I want to grow close to Him, so I practice the spiritual disciplines taught throughout these chapters. Intimacy with God is vital because obedience flows out of true love for God.

There will be days when I am tempted to follow my own ways. That is when accountability protects me. I need others who will hold me accountable to stay on track. These are prayer partners, not accusers. I need to gather a few trusted believers in Christ who will pray with me and ask me tough questions.

It is difficult for many to be open to others. We resist the idea of sharing our temptations and having them ask us how we handled those temptations each week. However, it is precisely in this kind of openness and accountability that we find true spiritual healing. "Therefore confess your sins to each other and pray for each other so that you may be healed. The prayer of a righteous man is powerful and effective" (James 5:16).

Ask God to give you the courage and wisdom to find trusted accountability prayer partners. Meet each week. Establish confidentiality. Agree to ask each other how you are handling specific temptations.

Caution: establish an accountability relationship with someone of the same sex. Most people find they develop a deep friendship with their prayer partner. Having a prayer partner who is the same sex can avoid confusing the deep friendship with sexual temptation.

Once you and your prayer partner establish rapport, trust, and confidentiality, get ready for God to take your spiritual walk to the next level.

SPIRITUAL JOURNEY JOURNAL

WEEK 15

Finish your personal plan for growth. Be honest with yourself about those areas where God is trying to stretch you. Begin identifying those who could serve as accountability prayer partners with you. Ask God to help you establish these very important relationships.

Now that you have tried the spiritual disciplines taught

throughout this book, take a few moments to review them. Which ones were most effective at helping you connect with God? Remember, the most effective practices may not be the easiest. Several of the disciplines are listed below in general categories. As you learn new disciplines, you can add them to these lists.

Prayer/Fasting	Bible Study	Worship	Journaling/ Self-Evaluation	Ministry to/ Serving Others
Breath prayers (chap. 1)	Bible study from sermons (chap. 5)	Using music (chap. 6)	Accountability prayer partner (chap. 15)	Ministry to the hurting (chap. 9)
Praying the Scripture (chap. 2)		Adjusting spiritual eyes (chap. 12)	Plan for growth (chap. 13)	Unseen acts of kindness (chap. 10)
The Lord's Prayer (chaps. 3 and 4)		Conflict resolution (chap. 14)		
Offerings/tithing (chap. 7)				
The hand (chap. 8)				
Fasting (chap. 11)				

Each week try to incorporate all the categories by doing at least one discipline from each. Assign a different discipline to each day of the week, or do the same set of disciplines each day. Find out what works best for you.

For your Spiritual Journey Journal this week choose one or two disciplines for each day of the week and list them below in the spaces provided. Keep in mind that many of these items are not optional for the believer. Just because tithing or prayer is difficult for you doesn't mean you can leave it out of your life.

Practice these spiritual disciplines *every* week . . .

*God's Tithe Is $*_____

My Place for Personal Worship Is . . .

My Time(s) for Personal Worship Is (Are) . . .

Monday

Spiritual disciplines to incorporate today:

1.

2.

Tuesday

Spiritual disciplines to incorporate today:

1.

2.

Wednesday

Spiritual disciplines to incorporate today:

1.

2.

Thursday

Spiritual disciplines to incorporate today:

1.

2.

Friday

Spiritual disciplines to incorporate today:

1.

2.

Saturday

Spiritual disciplines to incorporate today:

1.

2.

Sunday

Before leaving for church, ask God to draw near to you. Enjoy whichever spiritual disciplines you've chosen to incorporate into your day. Use the sections below to guide you on this Sabbath Day as you worship and spend time with God. Spiritual disciplines to incorporate today:

1.

2.

Insights from Sunday School/Bible Study/Small-Group Time:

Preparing for Worship:

During worship, I need You to do this in my heart . . .

As I come to worship, I need You to know . . .

Insights from Worship:

Reflecting on this Sabbath . . .

Today, God, You showed me . . .

This week I want You to do this in my heart . . .

Self-Evaluation—God's call to transformation:

KEEP GOING . . .

Now that your friendship with God is developing and you are well on the way to having His image restored in you, don't stop. Keep opening yourself up to Him through the practices described in the Spirit sections of this book; review the Truth sections from time to time; and in a notebook or on a computer continue writing your Spiritual Journey Journal. As you get to know God better, you will find many wonderful things happening in your life.

A time will even come when His love will overtake all you desire to do. This love will overflow from you back to Him and also into the lives of others. You will find yourself truly loving God with your entire being and your neighbor as yourself (see Matthew 22:37-40). But this is still not the end; there is much more to come. Your friendship with God will deepen, as will your knowledge about Him. Your growth will continue throughout your lifetime and beyond; it's an eternal journey.

So keep going. You're at the start of a magnificent adventure. At the end of one blessing is the beginning of another, and God has many blessings in store for you. Let Him lead the way as you continue your walk on this fabulous pathway that never ends.

APPENDIX

My Plan for Personal Growth

SPIRIT

1. Scripture and pray daily—first thing. Nothing else first.
2. Faith (my attitude)—constantly check myself to make sure I am trusting God for my answers.
3. Relationship with my spouse—schedule minimum once a week time with him or her (do on Sunday).
4. Pray through on number to win to Christ this year by end of March.

MIND

1. Read one chapter minimum each morning—right after prayer.
2. Refuse to use crude words.
3. Turn to God for help and quit pressuring other people.
4. Refuse to use debt spending.

BODY

1. Stay on track with my diet.
2. Exercise at gym Monday, Thursday, Saturday.

Weekly Activities for Spiritual Growth

Monday
Scripture and prayer.
Read one chapter.
6 A.M. go to gym.

Tuesday—Study and Spirit Day
Scripture and prayer.
Read one chapter.
Confirm date with spouse and line up baby-sitter.

Wednesday
Early morning prayer with accountability partner.
Read one chapter.
Wednesday evening Bible study.

Thursday
Scripture and prayer.
Read one chapter.
6 A.M. go to gym.

Friday
Scripture and prayer.
Read one chapter.
Reserve for family date night.

Saturday
Early morning prayer and breakfast with men.
Go to gym.
Spend afternoon with my family.

Sunday
Scripture and prayer.
Sunday School and church with family.
Schedule date with spouse.

Monthly Goals for Spiritual Growth

January   two books
              weight-225
              People I've Led to Christ:

February   two books
              weight-220
              People I've Led to Christ:

March   two books
              weight-215
              People I've Led to Christ:

April   two books
              weight-210
              People I've Led to Christ:

May   two books
              weight-205
              People I've Led to Christ:

June   two books
              weight-200
              People I've Led to Christ:

July   two books
              weight-195
              People I've Led to Christ:

August   two books
              weight-190
              People I've Led to Christ:

September   two books
              weight-185
              People I've Led to Christ:

October   two books
              weight-185
              People I've Led to Christ:

November   two books
              weight-185
              People I've Led to Christ:

December   two books
              weight-185
              People I've Led to Christ:

Next Year's Plan for Personal Growth

Notes:

My Plan for Personal Growth

SPIRIT

MIND

BODY

Weekly Activities for Spiritual Growth

Monday

Tuesday—Study and Spirit Day

Wednesday

Thursday

Friday

Saturday

Sunday

Monthly Goals for Spiritual Growth

January

February

March

April

May

June

July

August

September

October

November

December

Notes:

BIBLIOGRAPHY

Beasley-Murray, George R. *Word Biblical Commentary*. Vol. 36, *John*. Dallas: Word Books, 1998.

Freeborn, E. Dee, Wes D. Tracy, Janine Tartaglia, Morris A. Weigelt. *The Upward Call*. Kansas City: Beacon Hill Press of Kansas City, 1994.

Green, Joel B., Scot McKnight, and I. Howard Marshall. *Dictionary of Jesus and the Gospels*. Downers Grove, Ill.: Intervarsity Press, 1992.